Instructions for using AR

LET AUGMENTED REALITY CHANGE HOW YOU READ A BOOK

With your smartphone, iPad or tablet you can use the **Hasmark AR** app to invoke the augmented reality experience to literally read outside the book.

1. Download the **Hasmark app** from the **Apple App Store** or **Google Play**

2. Open and select the (vue) option

3. Point your lens at the full image with the and enjoy the augmented reality experience.

Go ahead and try it right now with the Hasmark Publishing International logo.

ENDORSEMENTS

"*Interior Designing for the Neurodiverse: A Transformational Guide* brings light with the value and knowledge of creating autism-friendly environments inviting a quality of life that embraces more calm, balance and harmony! The detail in this book offers an abundance of ideas and insight into the colors, texture, lighting, flooring, curtains, furniture, and so much more to design your own or your child's space to energetically connect to life. I truly believe *Interior Designing for the Neurodiverse: A transformation Guide*, directly syncs in with our mental health and wellbeing for the neurodiverse community and all!"

— Donna Laitinen,
Founder of Evoke Change Center, International Best-Selling
Author of *The Highest Frequencies of Love; Unconventional Solutions
for Parents of Children on the Autism Spectrum*; Speaker
and Behavior Change Specialist

"*Interior Designing for the Neurodiverse: A Transformational Guide* shows the intricate wiring of our brains, and that diversity goes beyond culture, religion and ethnicity. Author Dr. Maria Xirou takes us step by step in building a friendly environment for all".

— Mouna Saquaque Bestselling
Author of *Who Am I? Where Am I?* and *Back to Love and Beauty*

"**Dr. Maria Xirou** is a consummate professional and I am in awe of her vision. We have a family member who is neurodiverse and she combines her skills from her experience as a Consultant Paediatrician alongside her interior design abilities and it is such a powerful combination. The result is a home that now feels like "home" and a beautiful calm space for our loved one. Would not hesitate to use; Maria has seamless coordination and negotiation skills. We absolutely adore our new space and I am forever grateful".

— Sian Thomas

"I just wanted to thank **Dr. Maria Xirou** for her creative, understanding and collaborative design of my new apartment. She allowed me to embrace my preference for contemporary metal and glass, whilst gently augmenting their minimalistic beauty with luxuriously soft accessories. I would highly recommend her expertise".

— Dr Riyaad Sayed

"Author **Dr. Maria Xirou** demonstrates the importance of harmony in our homes and the spaces around us in *Interior Designing for the Neurodiverse: A Transformational Guide*. This book showcases the many ways we can reorganize our spaces in a mindful way to find balance and shift the energy in a positive way for the neurodiverse community and all".

— Judy O'Beirn
President of *Hasmark Publishing International*

INTERIOR DESIGNING FOR THE NEURODIVERSE
A TRANSFORMATIONAL GUIDE

DR. MARIA XIROU

Published by
Hasmark Publishing International
www.hasmarkpublishing.com

Copyright © 2024 Dr. Maria Xirou
First Edition

No part of this book may be reproduced or transmitted in any form or by any means, electronic or mechanical, including photocopying, recording or by any information storage and retrieval system, without written permission from the author, except for the inclusion of brief quotations in a review.

Disclaimer

This book is designed to provide information and motivation to our readers. It is sold with the understanding that the publisher is not engaged to render any type of medical, psychological, legal, or any other kind of professional advice. The content of each article is the sole expression and opinion of its author, and not necessarily that of the publisher. No warranties or guarantees are expressed or implied by the publisher's choice to include any of the content in this volume. Neither the publisher nor the individual author shall be liable for any physical, psychological, emotional, financial, or commercial damages, including, but not limited to, special, incidental, consequential or other damages. Our views and rights are the same: You are responsible for your own choices, actions, and results. This book is for educational and informational purposes only. The content of this book should not be interpreted as medical or professional advice. The reader should carefully evaluate the information provided and consult with a licensed health-care professional before making any decisions or taking any actions based on the content of this book. All the information has been checked to the best of our ability to be factually correct at the time of print. New research gets published often. This book does not replace a visit with your health-care provider. Do not ignore advice from your health-care provider because of something.

Permission should be addressed in writing to Dr. Maria Xirou at maria@xiroukatyalinteriors.com

Cover Design: Anne Karklins anne@hasmarkpublishing.com
Interior Layout: Amit Dey amit@hasmarkpublishing.com

ISBN 13: 978-1-77482-262-3
ISBN 10: 1-77482-262-8

Dedicated to my beloved husband, whose presence has not only transformed my perspective on life but has also been the unwavering pillar of support since the moment our paths intertwined. His love has illuminated my world with warmth and joy, and his unwavering dedication to this journey together fills my heart with profound gratitude.

M.X.

Words from the Author

Welcome to "Interior Designing for the Neurodiverse," a book that combines my passion and dedication working in the fields of paediatrics, mental health, and interior designing. Through my experience working with young people and their families, I've had the privilege to witness the unique strengths that neurodiverse and neurodivergent people bring, whilst recognising their difficulties and the significant challenges these can pose to their mental health and wellbeing. It is important to validate individual experiences within this vast spectrum of neurodiversity, ensuring their needs are met and their strengths are celebrated. I deeply believe the pivotal role of interior designing in promoting a more personalised perspective by embracing neurodiversity.

The neurodiverse conditions covered in this book are not exhaustive; rather, the ones illustrated represent just a selection of them.

For the purpose of this book, I use neurodiversity to reflect the diverse range of individual differences and experiences. I am aware that there are different ways and preferred terms to describe different neurodevelopmental differences, whilst different conditions or disorders are still defined according to their diagnostic criteria. Neurodiversity appears to me to be the most inclusive.

The spectrum of autism and other neurodevelopmental conditions are more varied and much broader. It is more helpful to understand individual strengths and needs across development. I hope this book serves as a valuable resource for anyone looking to design spaces that cater to a wide spectrum of needs, whether they identify as neurodivergent, neurodiverse, or are part of the community with more significant or profound needs. Drawing from my extensive professional experience in assessing and treating young people, I am hopeful that this book offers practical insights that transcend conventional definitions, ensuring inclusivity for all.

CONTENTS

FOREWORD	xvii
PART I: UNDERSTANDING NEURODIVERSITY	**1**
Chapter 1: The Multifaceted World of Autism Spectrum Disorder (ASD)	3
Chapter 2: The Kaleidoscope of Attention Deficit Hyperactivity Disorder (ADHD)	7
Chapter 3: Navigating Sensory Processing Disorder (SPD)	11
Chapter 4: Unravelling Developmental Coordination Disorder (DCD)	13
Chapter 5: Navigating a Unique Cognitive Landscape of Dyslexia	15
Chapter 6: Navigating Tourette's Syndrome and Tics	19
Chapter 7: Tackling Sleep Challenges	21
PART II: DESIGNING FOR THE NEURODIVERSE	**23**
Chapter 8: Colour Schemes - Physiology, History, and Psychology in Creating Neuroinclusive Environments	25
The Physiology of Colour Perception:	25
How Neurodiverse Populations Perceive Colours:	26
Historical Evolution of Colour in Interior Design:	26
Spiritual Significance of Colour in Different Religions:	26
Chromotherapy and Ancient Cultures:	27
Unique Healing Properties of Colours:	27
Colour Schemes for Neurodiverse Environments:	36
Chapter 9: Textures and Materials - Sensory Preferences and Practical Considerations	43
Chapter 10: Flooring Choices - Catering to Sensory Preferences and Mobility Needs	47

Chapter 11: Lighting - Enhancing Wellbeing for the Neurodiverse Population   51

Chapter 12: Acoustics and Sound Management - Enhancing Sensory Comfort   55

    Impact of Sound on Sensory Experiences: 55

    Solutions for Soundproofing and Acoustic Design: 56

Chapter 13: Furnishing and Layout of Interiors - Designing for Neurodiverse Needs and Preferences   57

    Furniture Selection: 57

    Layout Strategies for Different Neurodiverse Conditions: 58

Chapter 14: Mental Health and Interior Design   61

Chapter 15: Fostering Inclusive Environments – Real-Life Illustrations   63

PART III: PRACTICAL EXERCISES   67

Chapter 16: Understanding and Applying Neurodiverse-Friendly Design Principles   69

    Exercise 1: Reflection on Personal Experience   70

    Exercise 2: Exploring Neurodiverse Experiences   72

    Exercise 3: Exploring the Impact of Colour in a Room   74

    Exercise 4: The Importance of Lighting   75

    Exercise 5: Sensory Sensitivities   77

    Exercise 6: Apply What You Learned in Practice   79

PART IV: CULTIVATING NEURODIVERSE-INCLUSIVE DESIGN: RESEARCH, LITERATURE REVIEW, AND INSPIRATIONAL CASE STUDIES   83

Chapter 17: Research and Literature Review   85

Chapter 18: Existing Designs that Showcase the Importance of Neurodiverse-Inclusive Design Principles   89

CONCLUSION	**91**
Moving forward, there are several important steps to take:	93
APPENDICES	**95**
Glossary related to neurodiversity and interior design	97
Resources and recommendations for professional assistance:	101
ACKNOWLEDGEMENTS	**103**

FOREWORD

As Creative Director of lightiQ, working with interior designers and architects on luxury lifestyle projects it is always a delight to meet specialists in their fields as they bring a unique perspective, sharing their knowledge, pushing boundaries and delving deeper into the discipline of design. This insightful approach creates far reaching consequences for the community as a whole as new areas of expertise are incorporated into our awareness. Past examples of this would be biodynamic design and eco conscious recycling. I met Maria whilst lecturing at KLC School of Design and am so excited that a new path is being forged for the neurodiverse community.

Maria's lengthy career as a consultant paediatrician focusing on neurodiverse individuals brings a new perspective to the design agenda. The spaces we inhabit and the walls we call our home create the foundation for our daily lives, how we feel, how we approach each day, how we respond and react to others. A true home is many things, a sanctuary, a creative den, a calm space, an inspirational bolthole. Maria's 25 years experience in the specialist field of neurodiversity guides us with this enlightened and practical book.

Maria has gained an extraordinary insight into the unique world of neurodiversity and is well placed to share her authority on the subject. The book provides design guidance and is accessible to everyone, however, the ability to put it into action is down to you. To design is a verb, an action, it requires focus and energy, time dedicated to it, and this is often where clients fall down, and those who need the most help often lose the focus before really starting. Clients often do not spend enough time on their projects, or ask the right questions. This is where Maria's book will assist, taking you on a step by step journey, guiding you to the solutions which are right for you.

Maria and I have shared many funny stories of growing up with the challenges of feeling the world to be a certain way. I am the child who put masking tape down the middle of their bedroom so their sister could not clutter or infiltrate their side! My environment has always been so important to my sense of well-being which is why I understand the importance of getting the basics right. This often starts with natural light, then the room's usage, its furniture arrangement, followed by textures and colours. All of this is carefully outlined in Maria's book. As a lighting designer, I know that if I am struggling with the lighting plans I need to look at the layout and see if it can be improved. I have had many neurodiverse clients over the years who have challenged the traditional approach to lighting. I am a better designer because of it. The job of a great designer is to work through their client's needs, to really listen and the book provides practical guidance and case studies to assist you. If you have a neurodiverse child or family member whose well-being depends on their home, this book is for you.

Maria's book begins by outlining specific neurodiverse conditions and provides examples of patients, the second section navigates you through the tools to craft a nurturing space. Part three provides case studies and practical exercises to ensure your designs enhance the overall well-being and quality of life desired. Maria takes us through this on a step by step guide. However, always pragmatic, there is no one stop solution, we are all unique and our needs will be too.

Maria, has empathy and kindness in abundance and this shines through in her very calm approach. Maria's passion for interior design started at a young age, she was determined to be an architect and switched only at the last moment to being a doctor. Today her worlds merge! Dr Maria Xirou brings her wealth of specialist knowledge so we may craft thoughtful, holistic environments for the neurodiverse community.

Rebecca Weir, Creative Director of LightIQ

PART I:

UNDERSTANDING NEURODIVERSITY

CHAPTER 1

The Multifaceted World of Autism Spectrum Disorder (ASD)

Autism Spectrum Disorder (ASD), often referred to as autism or ASC (Autism Spectrum Condition), is a complex and multifaceted neurodevelopmental condition. It weaves a diverse tapestry of expressions and experiences, making it a unique journey for each individual. Autism primarily affects three core areas: communication, social interaction, and behaviour. The way these challenges manifest can vary significantly from person to person. In this chapter, we will embark on a journey to unravel the intricacies of ASD, understanding its various dimensions and the impact it has on those who experience it.

Imagine meeting Anna, a bright 20-year-old woman who received her ASD diagnosis two years ago. Anna's life has been marked by both challenges and triumphs. Her story serves as a compelling example of the diverse experiences within the spectrum. Anna's journey through the educational system perfectly illustrates the diversity of challenges experienced by individuals with ASD.

During her early years in a small primary school, Anna was a happy and well-loved student. Her teachers praised her, and life was relatively smooth. However, as she transitioned to secondary school, a storm of anxiety and overwhelm began to brew. Despite her academic excellence and impeccable behaviour, Anna felt different to the others, and struggled to adapt to the bustling environment. She concealed her inner turmoil so well that her teachers were unaware of her distress. Anna possesses a remarkable talent for art, capable of meticulously reproducing line drawings of objects she's only glimpsed once, and she excels at capturing human profiles. It was these creative pursuits that provided solace during her challenging years.

Anna shared her room with a very sociable young lady, and their constant stream of friends visiting in the evenings became a significant source of stress for Anna. Throughout her college years, Anna continued to mask her anxiety, eventually leading to her withdrawing from friends and colleagues.

ASD is like a vast mosaic, with each individual contributing their unique piece. Within this spectrum, people may grapple with difficulties in social communication, interpreting facial expressions, forming and maintaining friendships, and expressing their emotions and interests. Understanding others' thoughts and feelings can be challenging, and the world of social cues remains enigmatic. Processing new information often takes more time, and repetitive thinking and behaviours are part of daily life.

Sensory sensitivities add another layer of complexity. Bright lights, loud noises, peculiar textures, or overwhelming smells can trigger intense reactions. Predictability and routine become cherished anchors in a world that often feels chaotic. For many, any deviation from their meticulously structured routines can be deeply distressing. They take comfort in the stability of their belongings and can become upset when their order is disrupted.

Despite these challenges, autistic people have a great capacity for affection, sensitivity, and care. They can also exhibit remarkable focus on their interests and may have exceptional skills. With proper support, particularly during their early years, they can excel in their chosen fields. Well considered interior design choices can greatly reduce their challenges and help them thrive.

Some individuals with autism may exhibit challenging behaviours during childhood into late teenage years, which may include self-harming behaviour such as biting, hitting their head, or lashing out, sometimes resulting in harm to others. These behaviours tend to become more prominent in situations where these individuals experience anxiety, stress, or over-excitement.

It is crucial to recognise that not everyone with ASD will have all these difficulties. The presentation varies widely from person to person. Additionally, ASD frequently coexists with other conditions, such as gastrointestinal issues, epilepsy, learning difficulties, and mental health problems such as anxiety and depression.

Addressing the unique needs of individuals with ASD requires a holistic approach. This approach combines psychological interventions such as behavioural therapy, speech and language therapy, and occupational therapy, sometimes complemented by medication for other medical and / or mental health problems. However, the physical environment in which they live plays an indispensable role in their overall wellbeing.

In this book, we will explore how interior design can become a valuable tool for crafting nurturing spaces for individuals with ASD. We will delve deeper into ways to help them navigate their sensory sensitivities and promote their overall wellbeing within environments that prioritise their specific needs and comfort. As we journey through these chapters, we will discover the profound impact that thoughtful design can have on the lives of those with ASD, enhancing their quality of life and fostering a sense of belonging.

The colour and texture of tiles or other materials used in a property determine how strengths are enhanced and needs are supported.

CHAPTER 2

The Kaleidoscope of Attention Deficit Hyperactivity Disorder (ADHD)

Attention Deficit Hyperactivity Disorder, commonly known as ADHD, is a neurodevelopmental condition that causes a wide variety of challenges. It is characterised by inattention, impulsivity, and often accompanied by hyperactivity, all of which can significantly impact an individual's development and functioning. Individuals with ADHD can also have extraordinary skills and abilities. If they are well supported in their difficulties, they can thrive and excel in their talents.

Meet John, a 13-year-old boy who has been diagnosed with ADHD. His daily life is a rollercoaster, reliant on medication to help him manage his concentration and hyperactivity. John's world changes when his medication begins to wear off, typically an hour or so after returning home from school. Without it, he finds it nearly impossible to sit still, even for a simple meal. John has an older brother and a younger sister, and their home has accumulated a plethora of belongings over the years. This cluttered environment overwhelms John, causing him to become irritable and, at times, even aggressive. He lacks a designated space where he can retreat to regain his composure. To make matters more challenging, he shares his bedroom with his brother, whose disorganised room further exacerbates John's struggles. John's desk by the window is his sanctuary, the only place where he finds a semblance of calm. Yet, even there, concentration eludes him as distractions abound. John's teachers share their concerns with his parents about his constant irritability at school, where he appears calm when in solitude or in a structured setting but struggles to maintain focus in a busy classroom. As a result, he's fallen behind academically.

ADHD is a neurodevelopmental disorder that typically emerges in childhood and often persists into adulthood, causing social and professional challenges. One of its hallmark features is inattention, which might seem paradoxical since individuals with ADHD can indeed concentrate when something captivates their interest. However, maintaining focus on less engaging tasks becomes a daunting challenge. They may appear careless, make mistakes, and frequently forget things. Organisation, time management, and meeting deadlines become Herculean tasks.

Hyperactivity is another facet of ADHD. Individuals may fidget, squirm, or impulsively leave their seats. Restlessness often drives them to wander frequently, and they may find it difficult to participate in group activities or stay quiet. Excessive talking and interrupting others are common, as is an aversion to waiting their turn. Interestingly, sleep patterns vary within this population, with some struggling to sleep, while others need very little sleep and remain energetic throughout the day.

It is crucial to recognise that ADHD manifests uniquely in each individual. Some may experience both hyperactivity and impulsivity, leading to frustration as they grapple with wanting to do things right but finding it challenging as they struggle to wait and often rush through tasks. Establishing and maintaining friendships can be an uphill battle due to frequent boredom and restlessness.

Creating stability, routine, calmness, and serenity becomes essential for individuals with ADHD. Breaking tasks into smaller, manageable steps can alleviate feelings of overwhelm. Tools like planners, calendars, and digital applications help them track appointments and responsibilities. Combined with the right environment, ADHD can actually turn into a source of creative energy and increased productivity, much like the many vibrant patterns that a kaleidoscope can create.

Treatment options for ADHD include behavioural therapy, medication, or a combination of both. Co-existing conditions such as generalised anxiety, depression, low self-esteem, and oppositional defiant disorder may also need attention.

In the chapters to come, we will explore how interior design can create supportive environments for individuals with ADHD, emphasising structure, organisation, reduced distraction, and sensory considerations. By understanding their unique needs, we can foster a sense of calm and wellbeing within their living spaces.

Bookcases, when thoughtfully designed with impactful colours, can transcend their utilitarian purpose and become a striking feature of a room. By selecting hues that command attention, bookcases not only showcase their contents but also add a captivating visual element to the space. Bold and vibrant colours can infuse personality and energy, while rich, dark tones lend an air of sophistication. When strategically placed and colour-coordinated with the room's overall scheme, bookcases can transform into focal points, creating a sense of depth and intrigue. Thoughtfully chosen colours support neurodiverse individual's needs.

CHAPTER 3

Navigating Sensory Processing Disorder (SPD)

In simpler terms, think of Sensory Processing Disorder (SPD) as a traffic jam in the brain where the sensory signals are jammed and cannot be processed, and the responses don't quite match what the senses are experiencing. SPD can generally be divided into two groups: those who are hypersensitive and react strongly to stimuli, and those who are hyposensitive and underreact. These sensitivities can apply to one or more of their senses. An analogy that works well is the different-sized cups. Different senses have their own sized cups, for instance, an individual may have a small cup (easily over spilled or overwhelmed) for certain sounds, but a big cup (easily under stimulated) for touch or movements and hence needing to constantly seek out for these opportunities.

Meet Sebastian, a 45-year-old man who has grappled with significant sensory sensitivities throughout his life. Sebastian has an affinity for furniture made of metal and glass, an unconventional choice that might disturb others with sensory processing challenges. When dining out, he enjoys a variety of foods, but when he's in the kitchen, cooking chicken every time. Loud or sudden sounds, like doors slamming shut, footsteps thundering down the stairs, or someone raising their voice, deeply disturb him. In fact, even his neighbour's toilet flushing next door becomes an overwhelming sensory ordeal. To find peace, Sebastian sleeps with earplugs and adheres to a meticulously structured morning and evening routine. Recently, he had to uproot his life and move house due to the persistent noise of his neighbour's flushing toilet, which became an obsession and source of anxiety for him.

Sensory processing difficulties can impact various senses, including auditory, touch, smell and spatial perception and orientation. Sensory processing difficulties can affect the balance and space as well as coordination and the effects may extend to one or more senses simultaneously. Challenges can range widely and manifest in complex ways. For some, everyday noises or loud sounds become overwhelming or even painful. Textures, clothing tags, or certain fabrics can be irritating or uncomfortable, making them difficult to tolerate. Common smells or tastes that others find perfectly ordinary can feel overpowering or unpleasant. Bright lights and crowded spaces can become unbearable as well. Conversely, some individuals may exhibit little or no response to these stimuli, showing indifference even to extreme temperatures. They may seek constant sensory stimulation, needing to touch objects, displaying fascination with spinning items, or preferring strong smells and tastes. Restlessness may be a common trait among them.

The impact of sensory processing problems on daily life is profound and requires considerable effort to complete even simple tasks like doing household chores or getting dressed. Fine motor skills, such as using a pen or buttoning a shirt, can pose challenges. Balance and coordination issues, as well as difficulties with spatial awareness, may also be a part of the equation.

Sensory Processing Disorder can occur in isolation or coexist with other conditions such as ADHD or autism. Early intervention is crucial, and occupational therapists play a vital role, especially during a person's formative years. Sensory Integration Therapy equips individuals with activities and tools to enhance their effectiveness while performing daily activities. Strategic approaches help them manage their environment and increase their overall comfort.

In the chapters that follow, we will explore how interior design can cater to the unique needs of individuals with Sensory Processing Disorder, fostering environments that promote comfort, manageability, and a sense of wellbeing.

CHAPTER 4

Unravelling Developmental Coordination Disorder (DCD)

Developmental Coordination Disorder (DCD), also known as Dyspraxia, is a condition that takes a toll on gross motor and fine motor skills, motor planning, and execution abilities. These challenges significantly affect daily life and the capacity to perform routine tasks. While DCD typically emerges in early childhood, its effects can persist into adulthood if not adequately managed during the developmental years.

Meet Arun, an 11-year-old boy diagnosed with Developmental Coordination Disorder. Arun's mother expresses her concerns about his constant clumsiness and frequent injuries. Living in a small London flat, Arun often feels constrained and upset due to the lack of space. Their living room houses a large sofa and a coffee table with sharp corners perpendicular to Arun's usual path. As a result, he frequently stumbles and gets hurt. His mother notes that he seems oblivious to door frames and furniture edges, lacking spatial awareness. Additionally, Arun struggles with riding a bicycle and becomes visibly irritated when tasked with using a pencil at school, citing discomfort and pain. His legs and hands bear bruises, prompting the school to question the frequency of his injuries.

Problems with DCD can vary significantly between individuals. The hallmark of this condition lies in the challenges individuals face with gross motor skills like running and jumping, as well as fine motor skills like using scissors, writing with a pen or pencil, and handling utensils for eating or grooming. Children with DCD grapple with processing and integrating sensory and motor information, leading to difficulties with tasks like dressing, buttoning clothes, and tying shoelaces. Their struggles extend into hand-eye coordination, making activities such as catching a ball or participating in sports a formidable challenge. This impediment often translates to slow task completion and an increased likelihood of accidents, creating a sense of clumsiness.

DCD's impact extends beyond the physical realm, affecting emotional and social aspects of an individual's life. It places strains on familial and personal relationships, as individuals with DCD often experience frustration and anxiety due to their difficulties, which can contribute to low self-esteem. They are at a higher risk of being targeted by bullies in school or encountering difficulties in the workplace. These challenges can give rise to challenging behaviours and sometimes lead to decreased physical fitness, as individuals may avoid physical activities due to balance and coordination problems, potentially resulting in weight issues.

DCD frequently coexists with ASD and ADHD, compounding the challenges faced by individuals with these conditions. However, with the right interventions and support, those with DCD can make significant strides in their daily life. Occupational Therapy plays a pivotal role, equipping individuals with strategies to manage tasks both at home and in the workplace. While there may be no cure for DCD, adults with the condition can enhance their daily living skills. In some cases, Speech and Language Therapy can also be beneficial, aiding in the processing and integration of information. With appropriate support, individuals with DCD can lead fulfilling and successful lives.

It's important to note that sensory sensitivities can add an additional layer of complexity to the challenges faced by individuals with DCD, potentially leading to anxiety and feelings of isolation and difference from the majority of the population, which may contribute to depression. In the chapters that follow, we will delve into how interior design can create spaces that cater to the unique needs of individuals with DCD, fostering environments that promote comfort, accessibility, and a sense of belonging.

CHAPTER 5

Navigating a Unique Cognitive Landscape of Dyslexia

Dyslexia is a neurological condition that profoundly shapes how individuals perceive and interact with written language. Dyslexia affects the processing of written information, especially spelling, reading and writing. It's crucial to understand that dyslexia is not synonymous with low intelligence. In fact, many individuals with dyslexia are exceptionally bright, possessing a range of unique cognitive strengths.

One of the important aspects of understanding dyslexia is recognising the strengths that often accompany it. Dyslexic individuals frequently demonstrate exceptional creativity, a heightened capacity for special thinking and problem-solving skills.

Meet Iman, a 32-year-old woman who has lived her life with dyslexia, which shaped her journey in various ways. As a child, Iman's difficulties with reading became apparent during her early years in school. While her peers effortlessly picked up reading skills, she struggled to recognise letters and sounds. She often felt frustrated and anxious when asked to read aloud in class, fearing the judgment of her classmates and teachers. These early experiences with dyslexia affected her self-esteem and confidence, making her, question her own intelligence. As Iman entered her teenage years, her difficulties with dyslexia began to extend beyond the classroom. Homework assignments that required extensive reading and writing were a source of endless frustration. She would spend hours working on assignments that her peers completed in a fraction of the time. Despite her dedication and hard work, her grades didn't always reflect her true potential, which added to her feelings of inadequacy.

Iman's social life was also affected during adolescence. She hesitated to join clubs or extracurricular activities that required reading or writing, fearing embarrassment or judgment from her peers. This self-imposed isolation led to feelings of loneliness and a sense of missing out on the typical teenage experiences.

In her early twenties, Iman's difficulties with dyslexia persisted as she pursued higher education and entered the workforce. She worked twice as hard as her colleagues to compensate for her reading and writing challenges, often staying late at the office to complete tasks. While she excelled in her job due to her exceptional problem-solving skills and creativity, she still felt like she was constantly battling her own limitations.

Educational professionals, including teachers and special education specialists, play an important role in identifying and supporting students with dyslexia. Individuals with dyslexia benefit from several evidence-based interventions which can help them to develop essential reading and writing skills while improving on their strengths.

Dyslexia can sometimes lead to social challenges, as individuals may feel isolated or different from their peers due to their difficulties with reading and writing. Dyslexic individuals may experience a range of emotions related to their struggles with reading and writing. These emotions can include frustration, anxiety, embarrassment, and low self-esteem. Over time, these negative emotions can affect mental health and overall wellbeing.

Dyslexia can coexist with other conditions such as ADHD, which may further impact an individual's mental health. Sensory overload is also a common challenge for individuals with dyslexia. Addressing coexisting conditions is essential for comprehensive support.

Designing interior spaces with the neurodiverse individuals in mind, especially those with dyslexia, is a transformative journey toward greater inclusivity and accessibility. By understanding their unique cognitive landscape, capitalising on their strengths, and thoughtfully tailoring environments to meet their specific needs, interior designers can make a profound difference in the lives of those with dyslexia. In doing so, we create spaces that embrace the beauty of neurodiversity and empower all individuals to flourish.

The combination of orange and dark blue is a striking and dynamic pairing that brings together two contrasting yet complementary colours. The vibrancy of orange, with its energetic and warm character, harmonises beautifully with the depth and stability of dark blue. This combination effortlessly creates a sense of balance, where the intensity of each colour enhances the other.

CHAPTER 6

Navigating Tourette's Syndrome and Tics

Tourette's Syndrome is a neurological condition that is characterised by repetitive, stereotypical, and involuntary movements and vocalisations, aptly referred to as tics. Typically emerging during childhood, the intensity of tics and other associated symptoms tends to improve over time and may even vanish. While there is no cure for Tourette's syndrome, effective treatments are available to manage the symptoms.

Allow me to introduce Amanda, a 30-year-old woman living with Tourette's Syndrome and difficulties akin to those associated with ASD though undiagnosed. Her tics remain uncontrolled, while her anxiety continues to escalate. Amanda grapples with sleep issues, which significantly affect her daily life and professional endeavours. She shares a two-bedroom flat with her sister, who took charge of redecorating the entire space after they purchased the flat. This process was overwhelmingly stressful for Amanda. Amanda's sister's penchant for bright colours led to a bedroom colour scheme combining brown with accent hues of yellow and lime green. Amanda's room, now also cluttered due to insufficient storage, exacerbates the challenges she faces in daily life.

The hallmark of Tourette's lies in its tics, which often surface during childhood, peak in early adolescence, and tend to ameliorate as individuals transition into adulthood. These tics can manifest as physical, vocal, or a blend of both. Motor tics may encompass actions such as grimacing, twirling, head or limb jerking, eye rolling, blinking, or even involuntary touching objects or other people. Vocal tics, on the other hand, can include throat clearing, tongue clicking, grunting, coughing, or repeating words uttered by others.

Some tics, like head movements, can be physically uncomfortable, and their intensity tends to surge during moments of excitement, fatigue, illness, stress, or anxiety. Since Tourette's Syndrome typically emerges early in life, individuals with the condition may have encountered bullying during childhood, potentially affecting their self-esteem and confidence. Some may exert tremendous effort to control their tics in public, only to experience a surge of tics once they return home.

Support for Tourette's Syndrome must be tailored to each individual's unique needs, as its impact varies widely among those affected.

Individuals with Tourette's Syndrome may also have coexisting Obsessive-Compulsive Disorder, ADHD, or even learning difficulties, often accompanied by anxiety and depression. Anxiety is often related to tics and the anticipation of when the next tic might occur. Low mood can result from trying to cope with the condition. Sleep disturbances are not uncommon either.

Understanding the triggers and developing effective coping strategies is paramount for individuals with Tourette's Syndrome. These triggers may stem from specific situations, activities, emotions, or even interactions with others. Identifying these triggers can be challenging, making the use of a diary a valuable tool. Equipping individuals with a deeper understanding of their condition empowers them to better cope with their symptoms and reduce stress.

Behavioural therapies, including comprehensive behavioural interventions and habit reversal training, practising stress management and relaxation techniques such as yoga, meditation, and deep breathing, can significantly benefit individuals with Tourette's Syndrome. In some cases, medication may be necessary to help alleviate symptoms.

Participating in concentrated activities can effectively diminish the intensity of tics. Moreover, creating a tranquil environment can contribute to reducing the frequency of tics. Like other neurodiverse individuals, people with tics or Tourette's Syndrome can flourish in the right environment and reach their potential.

In the subsequent chapters, we will explore how thoughtful interior design can create spaces that cater to the unique needs of individuals living with Tourette's Syndrome, fostering environments that promote comfort, accessibility, and emotional wellbeing.

CHAPTER 7

Tackling Sleep Challenges

Sleeping difficulties often accompany the neurodiverse population, creating a range of sleep disorders that affect their overall wellbeing. Let's explore some common sleeping disorders that are associated with neurodiversity.

People with ASD frequently encounter sleep problems, particularly with falling asleep and staying asleep. They may wake up multiple times during the night, experience restlessness, or have heightened sensitivity to noise, sometimes waking up very early in the morning. These sleep issues in individuals with ASD can be linked to worries, anxiety, sensory sensitivities, or even epilepsy.

Individuals with ADHD also often grapple with sleeping difficulties. They tend to struggle with unwinding at the end of the day and falling asleep. Restless leg syndrome can further disrupt their sleep, causing discomfort and restlessness.

Additionally, Tourette's Syndrome and DCD can be accompanied by sleeping difficulties, such as trouble falling asleep, frequent night waking, and poor sleep quality.

Recognising the importance of sleep hygiene is crucial, especially for neurodiverse individuals. Poor sleep exacerbates their existing challenges, making it essential to establish good sleep habits that contribute to better mood, mental health, physical wellbeing, and cognitive function, including learning and memory.

Allow me to introduce you to Jane, a 32-year-old woman diagnosed early in life with Autism Spectrum Disorder, Attention Deficit Hyperactivity Disorder, and Insomnia. Jane is a highly intelligent and capable individual who has battled anxiety and depression since childhood. She takes medication for her ADHD and was recently prescribed sleep aids by a specialist. However, when I met Jane, it became evident that she was troubled.

To provide a better understanding of her living environment, Jane shared some videos of her home. Upon review, it became apparent that her surroundings were a significant contributor to her sleep issues. Jane resides in a studio in London, where she struggles to maintain tidiness due to the abundance of personal items and clothing. She also works from home two days a week, which adds to the chaos. Given her current emotional state, Jane finds overwhelming, the idea of moving to a more functional and calming space. Her studio lacks a comfortable sofa or armchair for relaxation, and her dining table with two unused chairs further adds to the sense of disarray. Jane has a single bed which is next to the small table with the chairs. Frustrated and sleep-deprived, Jane has recently taken sick leave due to her demanding job and sleepless nights.

In the following chapters, we will delve into the ways in which thoughtful interior design can help create a more soothing and functional living environment for individuals like Jane, offering solutions that address their unique needs and promote better sleep quality and overall wellbeing.

PART II

DESIGNING FOR THE NEURODIVERSE

Designing for the neurodiverse requires understanding of both interior design principles and the specific needs or preferences of neurodiverse individuals.

CHAPTER 8

Colour Schemes – Physiology, History, and Psychology in Creating Neuroinclusive Environments

Colours grace our world with beauty and significance. They play a vital role in our lives, manifesting in the rainbow after a dreary rain, the vibrant foliage of autumn, and the rejuvenation of green in spring.

As Pablo Picasso aptly put it, "Colours, like features, follow the changes of the emotions." Colours also have the remarkable ability to affect our feelings, emotions, and moods, ranging from instilling calm and relaxation to triggering anxiety and irritability. Our concentration levels can also shift with the presence of certain colours in our surroundings.

Recognising the profound impact of colours, interior designers and artists, acknowledge their importance in shaping our lives.

The Physiology of Colour Perception:

Our perception of colour is rooted in the intricate process through which our eyes receive light waves and convey them to our brain, where they are interpreted into the colours we perceive. Unlike many other species, humans perceive colours through specialized cells called cones, located in the retina behind our eyes. These cones are sensitive to red, blue, and green wavelengths. The overlapping responses of these cones to a variety of wavelengths enable us to see the full spectrum of colours. To illustrate further, the amalgamation of all colours creates white, while passing white light through a prism reveals the splendid rainbow spectrum. Natural sunlight, too, consists of multiple colours, each reflecting or absorbing differently when it strikes an object.

How Neurodiverse Populations Perceive Colours:

Neurodiverse individuals often experience colour perception uniquely or intensely. Conditions like Sensory Processing Disorder and Autism Spectrum Disorder can alter sensory processing, including colour perception. For instance, some neurodiverse individuals may find certain colours exceptionally bright and overwhelming, while others may exhibit heightened sensitivity to subtle colour variations. Understanding these physiological and neurological variations is paramount for interior designers striving to create inclusive spaces for the neurodiverse communities. By comprehending potential differences in colour perception among neurodiverse individuals, designers can tailor environments to provide comfort and accommodation for all residents, embracing neurodiversity.

Historical Evolution of Colour in Interior Design:

Colours have held a pivotal role in interior design throughout history, transcending cultural, technological, and aesthetic boundaries in different regions and eras. In ancient Egypt, the colour blue symbolised spirituality and supremacy, evident in ornate frescoes and decorative artifacts. In Renaissance Europe, red and purple denoted wealth and status among the upper classes. The modern era witnessed the emergence of colour theory, advocating for a broader spectrum and a more scientific approach to colour selection in interior design. The 20th century saw both minimalistic designs with neutral hues and subtle tones, as well as bold colour schemes inspired by the Pop Art movement. Today, the general population is more aware of the physiological and psychological impacts of colours. Interior designers now adopt a more experimental and inclusive approach to colours in their projects.

Spiritual Significance of Colour in Different Religions:

Colours hold spiritual significance in various religions and traditions, conveying deep theological and cultural meanings and eliciting profound emotional responses. For instance, in Christianity, purple symbolises penance and royalty, while white signifies purity, joy, and kindness. Hinduism associates saffron, red, and yellow with distinct meanings like purity, sensuality, and learning, and these colours are integral to temples and religious ceremonies. Buddhism attributes tranquillity and wisdom to the colour blue. Islamic art employs rich colours to embellish mosques, although the specific colours may vary across different cultural contexts within the Islamic world.

Chromotherapy and Ancient Cultures:

Ancient civilisations dating back to 2000 BC, such as the Chinese, Greeks, Indians, and Egyptians, recognised the therapeutic potential of colours. They practiced Chromotherapy, utilising light and heat to treat various ailments and restore bodily balance. Their intuitive use of light and heat as healing tools addressed conditions like injuries, pain, and lung infections. Chromotherapy, also known as Colourology, remains in use today as an alternative and holistic treatment.

Unique Healing Properties of Colours:

Each colour possesses unique healing properties.

Red:

Red stimulates both the body and mind, generating energy and excitement but can be overwhelming, potentially leading to defiance and aggression. Interiors with bright red hues, especially intense ones, can hinder relaxation.

Red, a colour with a rich and diverse palette, can have a significant impact on the sensory experience of interior spaces for individuals with neurodiverse conditions. From the warm, comforting tones of deep crimson to the vibrant and energetic shades of scarlet, each hue of red carries its own unique properties. Darker reds, such as burgundy and maroon, are often associated with feelings of warmth, safety, and cocoon-like comfort, making them ideal choices for creating cosy and secure environments. In contrast, brighter reds like vermilion and cherry can bring a sense of vitality and excitement, making them suitable for spaces that require stimulation and energy. Understanding the nuanced properties of different red hues allows interior designers to tailor environments to the specific sensory needs and preferences of neurodiverse individuals, ensuring that the spaces they create are both aesthetically pleasing and functional for their unique sensory profiles.

Pink:

Pink, a colour often associated with sweetness, playfulness, and warmth, can be a valuable addition to interior design for neurodiverse individuals. From the soft and gentle hues of blush to the vibrant and energetic shades of magenta and hot pink, each shade of pink carries its own unique properties. Lighter pinks, such as pastel rose and baby pink, often evoke feelings of calmness, nurturing, and comfort, making them suitable choices for creating soothing and inviting environments that promote relaxation. Brighter pinks like magenta and fuchsia can bring a sense of energy, creativity, and positivity to spaces, ideal for areas that require stimulation and a touch of whimsy. The versatility of pink allows interior designers to create environments that cater to the unique sensory needs and preferences of neurodiverse individuals, ensuring that the spaces they inhabit are not only visually appealing but also supportive of their emotional and sensory wellbeing.

Green and pink, a delightful pairing in interior design, offer a playful and refreshing combination. The crispness of green harmonises effortlessly with the softness of pink, creating a dynamic and balanced contrast. This lively combination can infuse spaces with a sense of vitality and charm. Whether used in equal measure or as accents to each other, green and pink together bring a youthful energy to interiors.

Green:

Green instils harmony, balance, and a sense of safety but can provoke irritability and anxiety when leaning toward yellow hues.

Green, a colour closely associated with nature and tranquility, offers a wide range of hues that can have a profound impact on the sensory experience of interior spaces for individuals with neurodiverse conditions. From the calming and restorative shades of sage and moss to the invigorating and refreshing tones of lime and emerald, each hue of green carries its own unique properties. Lighter greens, such as mint and pistachio, often evoke feelings of serenity, balance, and renewal, making them excellent choices for creating soothing and harmonious environments that promote relaxation and focus. On the other hand, brighter greens like lime and chartreuse can bring a sense of energy, creativity, and vibrancy to spaces, ideal for areas that require stimulation and a sense of vitality. Interior designers can harness the diverse range of green hues to tailor environments to the specific sensory needs and preferences of neurodiverse individuals, ensuring that the spaces they inhabit are not only visually appealing but also conducive to their wellbeing and sensory comfort.

Blue:

Blue impacts the body, induces calmness, serenity, and pain relief, albeit with a perception of coldness. It also stimulates mental processes.

There are different hues of blue. Sky blue is a light shade which creates optimism and tranquility. This blue can be used in nurseries, bedrooms, bathrooms as it creates a peaceful atmosphere. Another hue of blue which creates a calming environment is powder blue. Darker blue hues like navy blue, midnight blue and oxford blue help the concentration. On the other hand, aqua, turquoise, cerulean blue are bright colours. They do not necessarily help the short attention span, in contrary, on many occasions are distractive. Teal is a blend between the blue and the green. It creates calmness. Indigo and periwinkle are blue hues with a touch of purple and they again create calmness.

Blue, a colour known for its calming and serene qualities, offers a plethora of stunning combinations in interior design. Paired with whites and creams, blue creates a classic, airy ambiance that exudes tranquillity. On the other hand, when joined with bright yellows or vibrant oranges, it enlivens spaces with a fresh and energetic atmosphere. For a sophisticated look, deep blues can be elegantly paired with metallic accents like gold or silver. Blue also complements earthy tones like greens and browns, harmonising interiors with a natural and soothing appeal. Whether used as the dominant colour or as an accent, blue's versatility allows designers to craft a wide range of inviting and stylish interiors.

Brown:

Brown fosters a cosy and warm interior, adding a touch of luxury.

Brown is a versatile and earthy colour that offers a wide spectrum of hues, each with its own unique character and associations. Beige is a light and neutral shade of brown. It is a popular choice for wall paint, upholstery and flooring. Beige is soothing and creates a sense of warmth and simplicity in interior design. Tan is a mid-range brown hue that conveys a sense of comfort. Tan works well as a neutral backdrop and can be paired with a variety of colours and styles. Mocha creates warmth and can be used to create cosy and inviting atmospheres in living rooms and bedrooms. Caramel is a warm and sweet brown shade that adds a touch of richness and indulgence to a space. It is often used in kitchen and dining room designs to create a cosy and inviting ambiance. Sienna is a reddish-brown hue that evokes the warmth and beauty of natural earth tones. It can create a rustic and inviting feel in interior design, making it a popular choice for country and farmhouse styles. Chestnut is a dark and reddish-brown that creates elegance and depth. It is often used for wood finishes and furniture, adding a sense of sophistication to interiors. Coffee brown is associated with warmth and comfort and can create a cosy and inviting atmosphere in living spaces.

On the other hand, Taupe is a complex and versatile neutral that combines brown and grey undertones. It is known for its timeless and sophisticated appearance and can adapt to a variety of interior design styles. This hue of brown is great for interiors that need to be more neutral and creates a feeling of calmness. Bronze is a metallic brown hue often used for decorative accents and fixtures. It adds a touch of opulence and elegance to a space, making it a common choice for lighting and should be preferred over the gold colour, which can be overwhelming for some neurodiverse individuals. Bronze is also a good choice for hardware. Mahogany is a deep and reddish-brown wood tone that signifies luxury and tradition. It is often used for high-quality furniture and panelling, adding a sense of classic elegance to interiors. It is better if it is used in small quantities as it can be overwhelming.

Yellow:

Yellow triggers a range of emotions, promoting positivity, self-esteem, and confidence, but can also induce anxiety and low mood.

Yellow, a colour associated with sunshine and warmth, offers a spectrum of hues that can play a vital role in designing spaces that cater to the sensory needs of neurodiverse individuals. From the soft and soothing pastel yellows to the bright and invigorating shades of lemon and gold, each hue of yellow has distinct properties. Lighter yellows, like pale buttercream and soft pastels, can evoke feelings of calmness and serenity, making them excellent choices for creating tranquil and harmonious environments. On the other hand, bolder yellows such as sunflower and mustard can bring a sense of vibrancy and energy to spaces, ideal for areas that require stimulation and creativity. Designers can utilise the diverse range of yellow hues to create interiors that align with the unique sensory profiles of neurodiverse individuals, ensuring that the spaces they inhabit are not only visually appealing but also supportive of their specific sensory sensitivities and preferences.

Combinations with yellow can evoke various moods and styles. When paired with soft pastels like pale blues and gentle pinks, it exudes a charming and whimsical atmosphere. Alternatively, when matched with deep blues or rich purples, it can create a bold and vibrant contrast. Yellow also pairs gracefully with neutral tones like grey or beige, offering a sophisticated and timeless look. This versatility allows designers to harness the warmth and energy of yellow to craft diverse and captivating interiors tailored to their clients' preferences and needs.

Orange:

Orange sparks emotional and physical reactions, evoking happiness, increasing appetite, and stimulating social interaction, but in larger quantities can also lead to frustration and sadness.

Orange, a colour that combines the warmth of red and the cheerfulness of yellow, presents a versatile range of hues that can greatly influence the sensory experience in interior design for neurodiverse individuals. From the muted and earthy tones of terracotta to the vibrant and lively shades of tangerine and pumpkin, each hue of orange possesses unique properties. Earthy oranges, like terracotta and burnt sienna, often convey a sense of stability, grounding, and warmth, making them excellent choices for creating cosy and secure environments that promote a sense of wellbeing. Brighter oranges, such as tangerine and coral, can bring energy, enthusiasm, and creativity to spaces, making them ideal for areas that require stimulation and focus. By harnessing the various hues of orange, interior designers can craft spaces that cater to the specific sensory needs and preferences of neurodiverse individuals, ensuring that the environments they inhabit are not only visually pleasing but also conducive to their wellbeing and comfort.

Purple:

Purple imparts energy and enhances spiritual awareness but may lead to low moods with prolonged exposure.

Purple, a colour that has long been associated with royalty, luxury, and creativity, offers a diverse spectrum of hues that can play a significant role in designing spaces tailored to the sensory needs of neurodiverse individuals. From the deep and regal shades of royal purple to the calming and introspective tones of lavender and lilac, each hue of purple carries its own unique properties. Darker purples, such as eggplant and aubergine, often evoke a sense of opulence, sophistication, and mystery, making them suitable choices for creating cosy and elegant environments that promote comfort and introspection. Lighter purples like lavender and periwinkle can bring a feeling of tranquillity, relaxation, and creativity to spaces, making them ideal for areas that require a sense of calm and inspiration. By understanding the diverse range of purple hues, interior designers can craft environments that align with the unique sensory profiles of neurodiverse individuals, ensuring that the spaces they inhabit are both visually pleasing and supportive of their sensory sensitivities and preferences.

The importance of different hues in design cannot be overstated. Hues, with their varying shades and tones, possess the unique ability to set the mood, influence emotions, and define the character of a space.

White:

White eliminates distractions, clears the mind, reduces stimuli, and creates a fresh ambiance, though it can occasionally make the space feel sterile and cold. It may also reduce stimulation and brain activity.

White, often associated with purity, simplicity, and a sense of spaciousness, holds a unique place in interior design for neurodiverse individuals. While it may appear as a neutral or blank canvas, white encompasses a variety of shades and undertones, each with its distinct properties. Pure white, for example, can create an airy and open feel in spaces, making it an excellent choice for rooms where sensory overload needs to be minimised. Off-white and warm ivory tones can add a touch of cosiness and comfort without sacrificing the sense of space, making them suitable for creating serene and welcoming environments. However, the starkness of bright white may be too intense for some neurodiverse individuals, so it is important to carefully consider the specific sensory needs and preferences when using white in interior design. By judiciously selecting and combining various shades and textures of white, designers can create visually appealing, calming, and sensory-friendly environments that cater to the unique needs of those with neurodiverse conditions.

Grey:

Grey elicits feelings of sadness and drains energy with darker shades but can bring a sense of peace when using light grey.

Grey, a versatile and neutral colour, plays a crucial role in interior design for neurodiverse individuals by offering a spectrum of hues that can evoke a range of sensory experiences. From the soft and soothing shades of dove grey to the sophisticated and timeless tones of charcoal and slate, each shade of grey has its own distinct properties. Lighter greys, such as pale silver and pearl grey, often create a sense of tranquillity and neutrality, making them suitable for creating calming and serene environments that promote focus and relaxation. Darker greys like charcoal and gunmetal can add depth and sophistication to spaces, making them ideal for areas that require a sense of cosiness and intimacy. Grey is an excellent choice for wall or cupboard paint, and can effectively tone down and balance the overall look when using busy tiles, furniture, or accessories. The balanced and versatile nature of grey allows interior designers to craft environments that cater to the unique sensory needs and preferences of neurodiverse individuals, ensuring that the spaces they inhabit are visually appealing and conducive to their sensory comfort.

Black:

Black, the darkest of all colours, holds a unique place in interior design for neurodiverse individuals. While often associated with sophistication, elegance, and a sense of mystery, the use of black in interior design should be approached with care and consideration for the specific sensory needs of individuals with neurodiverse conditions. Black can create a dramatic and intense visual impact, making it suitable for accentuating certain design elements or creating a cosy, cocoon-like atmosphere in spaces that require a sense of security and intimacy. However, its darkness may also be overwhelming for some individuals, potentially exacerbating sensory sensitivities. Therefore, the judicious use of black, often as an accent colour or in combination with other hues, allows interior designers to strike a balance between creating visually appealing, sophisticated environments and ensuring sensory comfort for neurodiverse individuals. Careful consideration and customisation are key when incorporating black into interior design for this demographic.

Colour Schemes for Neurodiverse Environments:

Several colour schemes can be employed to create suitable environments for neurodiverse families. These include:

Complementary Colour Scheme:

In this scheme, colours that complement each other are chosen. This can create a balanced and visually pleasing environment.

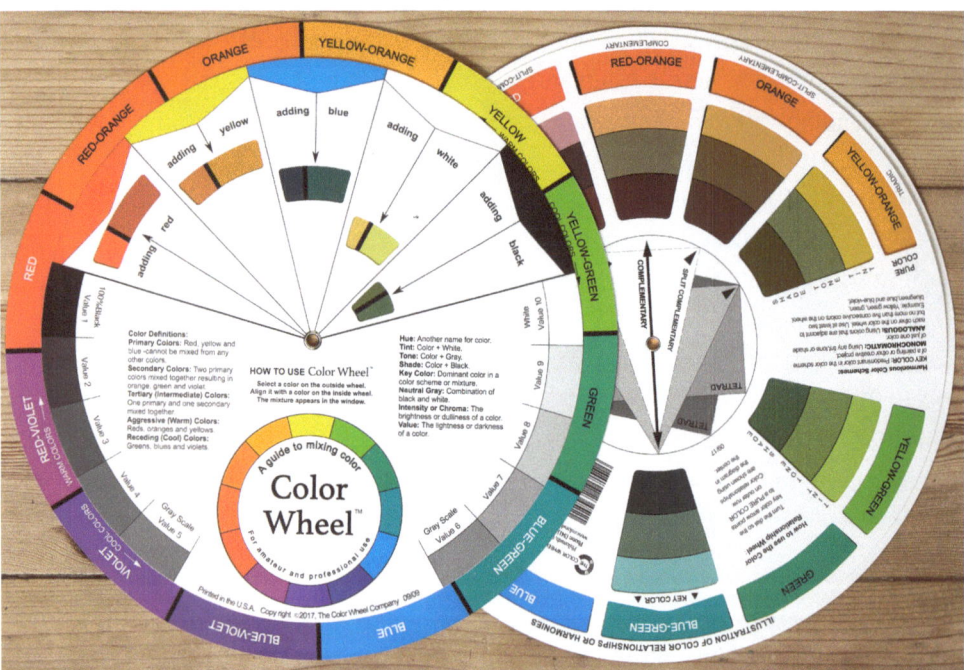

The colour wheel, a fundamental tool in interior design, provides a visual guide to selecting and harmonizing colours within a space. Designers rely on its arrangement of hues to create balanced colour schemes, evoke emotions, and strategically highlight focal points, ultimately enhancing the aesthetics and functionality of interiors.

Monochromatic Colour Scheme:

In situations where a single colour dominates the interior design, monochromatic colour schemes are utilised. These schemes are favoured for their simplicity and elegance, avoiding potential complexities and clashes that multiple colours can bring. Monochromatic colour schemes can be visually striking while maintaining a sense of cohesion. They can also incorporate accent colours for added interest and practicality.

The dominance of white and black hues, both within the monochromatic palette, and the absence of colour, as seen in the achromatic scheme, lends an air of sophistication and timelessness to the interior. This harmonious blend of tones not only appeals to the aesthetics but also recognises the significance of simplicity, elements that can have a calming and comforting impact on individuals with neurodiverse sensitivities, making the space both elegant and neurodiverse-friendly.

Monochromatic with Accent Colour Scheme:

A monochromatic with accent colour scheme is a design approach in which a single colour serves as the dominant or primary colour throughout a space. To create visual interest and contrast, a contrasting or complementary colour, referred to as an accent colour, is carefully introduced. This design concept achieves a balance between harmony and simplicity by predominantly featuring one colour while infusing touches of another to enhance depth and create focal points within the overall design.

A variety of accent colours can be introduced within monochromatic colour schemes to infuse character and elevate the ambiance. When employed in moderation, these accent hues have the power to invigorate the space without overwhelming it, ensuring a harmonious and visually appealing design.

Analogous Colour Scheme:

An analogous colour scheme involves using three adjacent colours on the colour wheel. These colours share a common base hue and are typically found next to each other on the wheel. Analogous colour schemes create a harmonious and pleasing visual effect, as the colours are closely related and share similar undertones. They are especially useful when aiming for harmony and avoiding strong contrasts or clashes between colours.

Choosing Colours according to the type of Neurodiversity:

Colours possess the power to significantly impact psychology and physical responses, with potentially amplified effects in neurodiverse populations. Here are some considerations when choosing colours according to different types of neurodiversity:

Autism Spectrum Disorder (ASD):

Opt for soft, muted colours like pastels, soft blues, light greens, and nature-inspired hues to create a calming environment and reduce sensory overload. In addition, darker blue and green hues as well as light grey hues and most hues of brown are a good choice for this community. Black in small quantities is also a good choice. Limit the use of bright and intense colours, as they can be overstimulating. However, individual preferences within the ASD community can vary widely, so consult with individuals with neurodiversity to meet their specific needs.

Attention Deficit Hyperactivity Disorder (ADHD):

Choose calming and neutral tones like beige, soft greys, earthy light greens, and soft blues to promote a sense of calm. Using dark blue in an office area helps the concentration. Darker and dull orange hues increase the concentration, as well as black in smaller quantities. Vibrant colours may increase restlessness and irritability. Be cautious with red, as it can be overwhelming and hinder relaxation. Lighter shades of red, like light pink, can create a calming effect.

Sensory Processing Disorder (SPD):

Create a soothing environment with muted, neutral colours and cool shades like light blue and light green. Avoid overstimulating neon colours and high-contrast colour schemes, as they can be overwhelming. White, light greys and beige hues are best for this population. Individuals with Sensory Processing Disorder have specific sensitivities to different colours and there is no other rule than to make sure that individuals are involved in the process of the choice of colours and decision making.

Dyslexia:

When it comes to colours, designers can opt for a palette that is both calming and conducive to reading and concentration. Neutral colours like beige and white provide a soothing background, reducing visual clutter and potential distractions. Additionally, soft and muted colours like light blue, gentle green, or subtle shades of pink can further promote a tranquil atmosphere, making it easier for individuals with dyslexia to focus on reading or other tasks. These colours not only provide visual comfort but also contribute to a sense of overall wellbeing.

Tourette's Syndrome and Tics:

Creating a welcoming and comfortable environment for individuals with tics is essential in interior design. Careful consideration of colour choices is paramount. Opt for soothing shades like gentle browns, soft blues, subtle greys, and delicate pinks. Green hues, except those leaning towards yellow, are also excellent choices. However, it's crucial to steer clear of vibrant yellows, which can induce anxiety and exacerbate tics. Similarly, bright oranges and fiery reds should be avoided as they can provoke stress and overwhelm. On the other hand, light pink can be a calming and supportive colour choice for individuals dealing with tics.

Sleeping Difficulties:

When it comes to creating a tranquil and sleep-friendly bedroom for individuals with sleep difficulties, thoughtful colour selection plays a pivotal role. Opt for calming options such as serene light blue, soothing shades of green, comforting beige, gentle light brown tones, peaceful light pink, serene off-white, timeless ivory, and soft light purple. These colours can work wonders in promoting a restful atmosphere, helping individuals find the peaceful slumber they need.

Co-Morbidities:

Addressing co-morbid conditions is essential. For individuals with light sensitivities and migraines, opt for matte colours to minimise glare and cool colours to reduce eye strain.

Anxiety: Opt for calming colours like blue, earthy greens, pastels, and neutrals to induce tranquillity. Steer clear of bright and warm colours like red, yellow, and orange, which can trigger tension and unease.

Depression: Black, dark blue or any blue in large quantities are actually not good choice for individuals suffering with low mood. Remember small quantities of yellow, red, orange can create a cheering atmosphere, but if yellow or orange is in larger quantities then this can worsen low mood and create anxiety. Purple must be used very carefully as it is a risk of mood deterioration. On the other hand, light pink hues can create a jolly and pleasant environment for individuals who suffer with low mood. Light blue creates a calming environment, but incorporating small quantities of colourful accessories or furnishings, such as vibrant cushions, can uplift the mood

Remember that individual preferences within specific neurodiverse groups can vary widely. The choice of colours should be based on individual needs and feedback, ensuring functionality, comfort, and overall wellbeing.

CHAPTER 9

Textures and Materials – Sensory Preferences and Practical Considerations

In the neurodiverse community, certain textures and patterns can trigger sensory overwhelm, distress, or distraction. Personalisation and customisation play a crucial role in creating comfortable and wellbeing-oriented spaces. Allowing individuals to select textures they find appealing fosters a sense of ownership and comfort in their environment. Incorporating personal touches like cushions and blankets can make a space feel inviting and secure.

Noise Absorption Materials:

For individuals with auditory sensitivities, it's essential to consider materials which dampen the noise while helping to minimise it's amplification. Upholstered furniture such as sofas, armchairs, and stools can absorb sound effectively. Thick carpets and curtains also contribute to noise reduction. By incorporating these noise-absorbing materials, you create a more serene and comfortable environment for those with sensory sensitivities.

Safety and Comfort:

In areas where gentle tactile experiences are needed, opt for furniture with rounded and smooth edges. This reduces the risk of injury and ensures a safe environment.

Maintenance and Cleaning:

When selecting fabrics and materials, take into account the ease of maintenance and cleaning. Choose materials that are easy to clean and maintain to ensure a hygienic living environment.

Choosing Fabrics for Neurodiverse Environments:

Selecting the right fabrics for neurodiverse populations, particularly those with significant sensory sensitivities, requires careful consideration. Here are some fabric recommendations:

Bedding: Soft cotton with a high thread count is an excellent choice for bedding. Higher thread counts tend to be more comfortable for the skin and durable due to tightly woven threads. However, they may be less breathable. Opt for a mid-range thread count (around 300-400) for a good balance between breathability and comfort, especially for individuals with temperature sensitivities.

Pillows: Hypoallergenic pillows are the preferred choice. Additionally, consider weighted blankets for individuals with sensory sensitivities, as they find them comforting and conducive to relaxation and sleep.

Furniture: Soft, smooth fabrics like cotton or soft wool are pleasant to touch and suitable for furniture like sofas and armchairs. Be aware that some individuals may not like fabrics such as velvet or silk, as they can evoke discomfort. Synthetic fabrics that irritate the skin should also be avoided. Wool, while warm, may not be suitable for individuals who feel warm constantly. Leather can have a cool sensation, so if it's chosen, opting for warmer colours may be more suitable. Keep in mind that sensory sensitivities are highly individual, and preferences vary widely.

Curtains: Opt for soft-textured, smooth, and lightweight curtain fabrics that diffuse light without causing excessive brightness. Consider using double curtains to provide flexibility for individuals with light sensitivities, allowing them to adjust the level of incoming light.

Carpets and Rugs: Choose carpets with shorter fibres to prevent tripping and falling, making them a great choice for individuals with Developmental Coordination Disorder or those who are clumsy. Short-fibre carpets are also easier to clean, which is crucial for many neurodiverse individuals. Use soft-textured and non-looped rugs to prevent catching toes, as some neurodiverse individuals prefer to be barefoot. Ensure that rugs and carpets are secured to prevent slipping.

Leather, when used in furniture such as chairs and sofas, adds a touch of timeless luxury and durability. Renowned for its natural elegance and resilience, leather upholstery not only offers a sophisticated aesthetic but also boasts properties like strength and longevity. However, it's important to note that some individuals may have sensitivities to leather due to allergies or preferences for vegan alternatives. In such cases, considering alternative upholstery materials becomes essential to ensure the comfort and well-being of everyone using the furniture. Leather furniture, when chosen mindfully, can effortlessly complement a variety of design styles, making it a versatile choice that combines both aesthetics and practicality.

Therapeutic Textures:

Soft and pleasant fabrics can have a therapeutic effect. Consider incorporating soft cushions, throws, bean bags, and tactile panels into the environment. These elements can provide a calming and soothing sensory experience. Avoid wall textures that are rough to the touch or create unexpected shadows, as they can be unsettling.

Pattern Selection:

When choosing patterns, be mindful of their potential impact on individuals with sensory sensitivities. Avoid wallpapers or fabrics with overly intricate designs or busy patterns, as they can be distressing. Patterns like paisley, densely packed floral patterns, and high-contrast stripes (especially when closely spaced) can be visually overwhelming. Irregular or varying-sized dense polka dots may also cause sensory discomfort.

Simple and Muted Patterns:

Opt for simpler, muted patterns to create a visually comfortable environment. Complex geometric patterns can appear to shift or move, which may be distracting or discomforting. Patterns with no clear focal point can prevent the eyes from resting, leading to feelings of unease. Moiré patterns, due to their visual effects, can also be distracting and should be avoided.

By considering the sensory preferences and practical needs of individuals in the neurodiverse community, you can create environments that are both comfortable and supportive of their wellbeing. The chapters that follow will delve further into design strategies that cater to the unique sensory experiences and sensitivities of neurodiverse individuals, fostering spaces that promote calmness and overall mental and emotional wellbeing.

CHAPTER 10

Flooring Choices – Catering to Sensory Preferences and Mobility Needs

When selecting flooring for the neurodiverse community, it's essential to consider a range of preferences and needs that can arise from sensory sensitivities and mobility issues.

Carpet Flooring:

Carpets come in various materials, styles, and types, each with its own set of advantages and disadvantages. Consider factors such as durability, comfort, and ease of cleaning when choosing the right carpet for each individual's needs and budget.

Low Pile Carpets: These have short, tightly woven fibres and are sturdy and easy to clean. They are ideal for high-traffic areas.

Medium Pile Carpets: Featuring longer fibres, medium pile carpets provide a cushioned feel while still being fairly easy to clean.

High Pile Carpets: These carpets have long, loose fibres, offering exceptional softness and comfort. However, they are harder to clean and are better suited for low-traffic areas.

Carpets have several benefits, such as reducing noise from footsteps and echoing, providing warmth and insulation against cold weather, and offering a comfortable surface for walking barefoot. They are particularly useful for individuals with sensory sensitivities and those who spend time on the floor. However, carpets can also collect dust and allergens, making them less suitable for those with allergies. They are also less durable than other flooring types and can fade more quickly, especially in high-traffic areas.

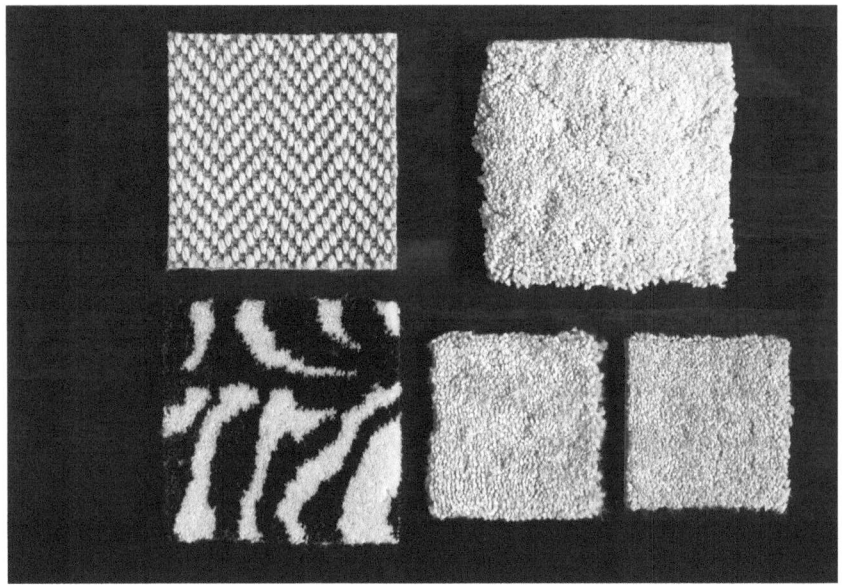

The variety of carpet options depicted in this photo underscores the significant impact of carpet choices on a space. From plush and thick carpets that evoke comfort to sleek, low-pile options that offer easy maintenance, each type of carpeting brings its own character and functionality to the environment. Carpet selection plays a pivotal role in shaping the visual appeal, acoustics, and overall comfort of a space, making it an essential factor to consider when planning any interior design project

Hardwood and Laminate Flooring:

Hardwood and laminate flooring are known for their durability and can last many years with proper care. They are easy to clean and are recommended for individuals with allergies. Hardwood floors have a natural look and can be aesthetically pleasing and calming. However, they are not suitable for individuals sensitive to noise, as they can amplify sounds. Additionally, hardwood and laminate floors can be uncomfortable to sit or lie on for extended periods.

If hardwood or laminate flooring is chosen, rugs can help mitigate noise and provide cushioned areas. It's essential to consider the characteristics of individuals with Developmental Coordination Disorder (DCD) when using these types of flooring, as they can be more susceptible to slipping and falling. Non-slip finishes and heavy rugs can help address this concern.

The diverse selection of flooring options showcased in this photo demonstrates the significant influence of flooring choices on a space. From the timeless appeal of wooden floors to the practicality of laminate and variations in thickness, each type of flooring offers a unique blend of aesthetics, durability, and maintenance requirements. The choice of flooring can greatly impact not only the visual appeal but also the practicality and feel of the space, making it a vital consideration in any design project.

Vinyl and Linoleum Flooring:

Vinyl and linoleum flooring are highly durable and resistant to water and wear. They are softer than hardwood or laminate, which can be less damaging to the body during falls. These materials offer a wide variety of designs and patterns, including wood and stone mimics. However, some vinyl floors can emit volatile organic compounds (VOCs), making them unsuitable for those with such sensitivities unless low VOC or VOC-free options are used.

Ceramic or Porcelain Tiles:

Ceramic and porcelain tiles are water-resistant and, in some cases, very durable. They are easy to maintain and clean. However, they feel cold and hard and can be uncomfortable for prolonged sitting. These tiles may not be suitable for individuals with auditory sensitivities, but the noise can be reduced with thick rugs or carpets. On the positive side, their cool surface can be considered for individuals with temperature sensitivities.

For individuals with sensory sensitivities, the choice of tiles in interior spaces can play a crucial role in creating a comfortable and accommodating environment. Busy tiles, characterised by intricate patterns, bold colours, and contrasting textures, may pose challenges for those with sensory sensitivities. The visual complexity of busy tiles can be overwhelming and even distressing for some individuals, contributing to sensory overload and discomfort. In contrast, simpler and more neutral tiles, with their clean lines and muted colours, are often preferred by individuals with sensory sensitivities as they create a calmer and less stimulating environment. The choice of tiles needs thoughtful consideration when designing spaces to be inclusive and accommodating for those with sensory sensitivities.

Cork Flooring:

Cork flooring reduces noise transmission, provides thermal insulation, feels warm to the touch, and offers a soft and cushioned surface. However, cork is not a strong material and can be susceptible to dents or punctures. It is comfortable for sitting and can be suitable for rooms where sitting on the floor is a preference.

Considerations for Comfort and Mobility:

Tactile sensory sensitivities play a crucial role in flooring choices. Low pile and tight-weave carpets are ideal for mobility devices and reduce tripping hazards. Carpet tiles can be an excellent choice in high-traffic areas as they are replaceable if damaged or stained.

A smooth transition between different types of flooring is vital to prevent trips and falls, especially when using mobility aids like walking frames or wheelchairs.

For individuals who may be clumsy or have coordination and balance issues, opt for hardwood flooring with a matte finish instead of a glossy one. Rugs can provide cushioning and protect such individuals from hurting themselves during falls.

Vinyl, linoleum, and glossy ceramic or porcelain tiles can be slippery when wet, making them unsuitable for clumsy individuals, including those with ASD and DCD. Consider textured options or alternative flooring types to reduce the risk of slipping.

From a visual sensory perspective, it is preferable to use neutral flooring or flooring with subtle patterns, as highly patterned options can be overstimulating and overwhelming. Furthermore, red, bright orange, or dark wooden floors may be overwhelming and may not be suitable choices for neurodiverse individuals.

Natural materials like stone and wood, especially with smooth finishes, can have a calming effect. However, the needs and preferences of each individual in the household should be considered, not just those who are neurodivergent, to achieve a comprehensive understanding of the household's actual needs.

CHAPTER 11

Lighting – Enhancing Wellbeing for the Neurodiverse Population

Lighting is a crucial element in interior design, with a profound impact on individuals, especially in the neurodiverse community. As mentioned earlier in this book, sensory stimuli and sensitivities can vary significantly among neurodiverse individuals. Therefore, it's essential to consider a wide range of factors when choosing appropriate lighting for their spaces.

Natural Light: Natural light is therapeutic, calming, and should be maximised whenever possible. It is generally softer and less intense than artificial lighting. Exposure to natural light during the day helps regulate circadian rhythms, improve mood, concentration, and sleep patterns. Large windows, skylights, and open layouts can maximise natural light. Sheer curtains or light blinds can also help increase the amount of natural light entering a space.

Colour Temperature: The colour temperature of light can affect mood and wellbeing. Warmer tones, with yellow hues, can be calming and comforting, while cooler tones, with blue hues, can be more uplifting and energising but may affect sleep patterns. Selecting the appropriate colour temperature based on individual preferences and sensitivities is essential.

Sensitivity to Light Changes: Many neurodiverse individuals are sensitive to sudden changes in light levels throughout their homes. Avoiding abrupt transitions between light and dark areas is crucial. Individuals with a history of epilepsy may experience significant discomfort with strong or sudden changes in light, particularly if their seizures are not well controlled. Fluorescent lighting is generally distracting and distressing and should be minimised, as it can be bothersome due to the humming and flickering associated with it. Always consult with neurodiverse individuals as some neurodiverse people may find these lights soothing.

Dimmable and Task Lighting: Dimmable lights offer flexibility, allowing individuals to adjust the lighting to their specific needs and comfort levels. Dyslexic individuals can benefit from adjustable lighting options, that can contribute to a more comfortable and focused environment. Other neurodiverse individuals may prefer dimmer lighting to prevent sensory overload, while others may need brighter lighting for specific tasks. Task lighting, such as wall-mounted lights for reading in bed, can be used to address task-specific lighting needs without overpowering the entire space. The concealed ceiling lighting imparts a soothing ambiance without overwhelming the space providing the perfect setting for relaxation. Lighting inside wardrobes and various cupboards is beneficial for neurodiverse individuals, particularly those with ADHD and Sensory Processing Disorder.

Incorporate lighting within wardrobes and storage areas to facilitate easier retrieval of items

Minimising Glare: Reflective surfaces, such as worktops and backsplashes, can cause glare, leading to visual strain and discomfort. Using matte finishes and strategic light placement can help minimise reflections and glare.

Tiles have the potential to reflect light, which may be discomforting for individuals with light sensitivities.

Night Time Lighting: Proper lighting during night time hours is essential. Reduced-power lighting along corridors and stairways can help individuals navigate safely during the night without disrupting sleep patterns. Some neurodiverse individuals, especially those with Sensory Processing Disorder (SPD), may be prone to trips and falls, especially at night. Battery-operated lights for stairways are a practical and cost-effective alternative when traditional lighting is not feasible. Consider LED motion sensor night light, which is USB rechargeable. This versatile lighting solution is perfect for illuminating hallways, cabinets, closets, wardrobes, stairs, bedrooms, kitchens, and basements.

Consulting Specialists: Given the wide range of lighting sensitivities and preferences within the neurodiverse population, interior designers and architects should work closely with their clients and, if necessary, consult specialists to ensure that the chosen lighting design aligns with the individual's unique needs and preferences.

Sleep Considerations: Adequate sleep is crucial for neurodiverse individuals, many of whom may struggle to fall asleep or stay asleep. Exposure to natural light during the day can improve sleep quality by regulating circadian rhythms. Large windows in areas with the most natural light exposure can be beneficial. Avoiding blue light in the evening and night is also essential, as it can interfere with the production of

The right lighting can transform a dining room into an inviting and memorable space.

melatonin, a hormone responsible for regulating the sleep-wake cycle. Additionally, avoiding shiny or glossy finishes on surfaces like worktops, backsplashes, walls, and flooring can create a calmer and more soothing environment. Intense colour combinations, such as bright neon colours or vibrant juxtaposed colour combinations, can be harsh on the eyes and should be carefully considered based on individual preferences.

In conclusion, lighting is a critical element in creating comfortable and supportive environments for neurodiverse individuals. Careful consideration of natural light, colour temperature, sensitivity to light changes, dimmable lights, glare reduction, and sleep considerations can lead to a more accommodating and pleasant living space. Consulting with specialists when necessary ensures that the lighting design is tailored to the individual's unique needs and enhances their overall wellbeing.

Practicing consistent bedtime and wake-up times, creating a peaceful sleep environment with minimal noise, engaging in regular exercise, limiting screen time before bed, and avoiding heavy meals and caffeine are some strategies that can be employed to promote better sleep.

CHAPTER 12

Acoustics and Sound Management – Enhancing Sensory Comfort

Sound has a significant impact on sensory experiences, especially for individuals in the neurodiverse community. Many neurodiverse individuals have heightened sensitivities or unique auditory processing patterns that can affect their comfort and functioning in various environments. Research showed that lower sound levels below 50 dB are conducive to autistic individuals' comfort. Here's an overview of the impact of sound on different experiences and effective solutions for soundproofing and acoustic design:

Impact of Sound on Sensory Experiences:

Sensory Overwhelm and Sensory Overload: Certain sounds or the accumulation of background noise can be overwhelming and lead to sensory overload and distress, particularly in autistic individuals, individuals with dyslexia and those with sensory processing difficulties.

Difficulty Concentrating: Unrelated background sounds can be highly distracting for individuals with ADHD, making it challenging for them to concentrate on their tasks.

Anxiety and Panic Reactions: Some neurodiverse individuals with auditory processing difficulties may struggle to process auditory information effectively, especially in noisy environments. Very loud or sudden noises can trigger strong physical reactions, such as severe anxiety or panic attacks.

Sleep Disturbances: Noise can disrupt sleep patterns, particularly for those who are more sensitive to sound.

Solutions for Soundproofing and Acoustic Design:

Use of Soft Materials: Soft materials like rugs, carpets, upholstered furniture, acoustic panels, and soft wall hangings or drapes can absorb sound waves and reduce echoes within a space.

Acoustic Diffusers: Acoustic diffusers scatter sound waves rather than absorbing them, reducing echoes and creating a more even sound in the room. These can be achieved using acoustic diffuser panels, irregular surfaces, bookshelves, or staggered wall structures.

Isolation Barriers: To isolate specific areas and prevent sound from traveling from one space to another, use acoustic doors, seals for gaps in doors and windows, double or triple-pane windows, insulated walls, underlay to reduce sound transmission, or floating floors.

Ambient Sound Generators: Devices that generate consistent ambient sounds can help drown out jarring intermittent noises, creating a soothing atmosphere and aiding concentration for some individuals.

Decoupling: Separating building materials to prevent sound waves from easily passing through them. This can be achieved with the use of resilient channels on walls, floating walls or ceilings, specialised clips, and hangers for drywalls.

Sealing Gaps: Seal all gaps in floors, walls, and ceilings where sound can pass through, including light fixtures and electrical outlets, which can be potential weak points.

Room-in-a-Room Concept: In situations where a soundproof room needs to be created, constructing a room within a room adds an additional layer of sound barrier.

Acoustic Furniture: Some furniture is designed with acoustic principles in mind, such as high-backed sofas and booths, providing privacy and a degree of sound absorption.

Landscaping: Outside elements like trees, plants, and hedges can act as natural barriers to sound. Water features like small waterfalls or fountains can provide pleasant sounds that mask more disturbing surrounding noises.

In conclusion, sound management and acoustic design are essential considerations when creating environments that cater to the sensory needs and comfort of neurodiverse individuals. Understanding the specific sensitivities and preferences of each individual is key to implementing effective soundproofing and acoustic solutions that enhance their overall wellbeing.

CHAPTER 13

Furnishing and Layout of Interiors – Designing for Neurodiverse Needs and Preferences

Designing interiors for individuals with neurodiversity requires a deep understanding of their unique difficulties, sensitivities, and preferences, which can vary widely across the population. As emphasised earlier, engaging in a meaningful discussion with the neurodiverse person and their caregivers or professionals is invaluable before making any design decisions or starting any work.

Furniture Selection:

The choice of furniture plays a crucial role in creating a comfortable and safe environment for individuals with neurodiverse conditions:

Sturdy and Safe Furniture: For individuals with coordination, balance, or motor challenges, as well as those with uncontrolled movements like dystonia and epilepsy, or challenging behaviour and self- harming, sturdy furniture is essential. These pieces are less likely to move easily or tip over, reducing the risk of accidents. It is advisable to avoid furniture made from glass or furniture like coffee tables with sharp metal corners in households where individuals with sensory processing disorder, epilepsy, or uncontrolled movements such as dystonia are present.

Low VOC or Non-VOC Furniture: Many individuals in the autism community are sensitive to smells and certain chemicals used in furniture. Choosing furniture made from natural materials or low VOC or non-VOC options that do not use formaldehyde glues or finishes can help create a more comfortable living environment.

Soft Furnishings: Chairs and sofas with softer fillings provide comfort and are preferred for individuals with sensory sensitivities. Avoid itchy or rough materials, as they can be irritating and distressing.

Quiet Furniture: Furniture with features like soft-close cabinets and drawers can significantly reduce sudden loud noises, which can be distressing for some individuals.

Storage Units: Labelled cupboards and drawers are excellent organisational furniture pieces, particularly beneficial for individuals with ADHD. They help in creating structured and organised living spaces.

Layout Strategies for Different Neurodiverse Conditions:

Neurodiverse individuals have a spectrum of needs and preferences. Here are some layout recommendations to enhance their living spaces:

Clear Pathways: Ensure that the layout includes clear walking pathways to accommodate individuals with coordination, balance difficulties, and mobility issues. Consider the height of each individual or wheelchair user to make sure items are within reach.

Consistent Layout: Many individuals with Autism Spectrum Disorder appreciate a consistent layout that remains the same and does not change frequently. This helps create a sense of stability and comfort in their home environment.

Safety and Accessibility: These are paramount, particularly for individuals with coordination and balance difficulties, mobility challenges, or disabilities. Interior designs should be free of trip hazards, incorporate handrails as needed, and consider accessibility in layout and furniture choices.

Calming Retreats: Designate calming, cosy areas within the home where individuals can retreat to when feeling overwhelmed. These areas can be decorated with cushions, throws, and candles of their preference, creating a retreat-like atmosphere that promotes relaxation.

Sensory rooms: The sensory room is a meticulously crafted haven designed to cater to the specific sensory needs of individuals, especially those who are neurodiverse. It's a space where every detail, from the colour scheme to the lighting, furniture, and textures, is thoughtfully selected to create a comfortable and soothing environment. Soft, calming colours dominate the room, creating a visually serene backdrop. Adjustable lighting allows occupants to control brightness and warmth, accommodating their sensory preferences. Plush, tactile materials and furnishings offer a sense of cosiness and security, inviting touch and interaction. In this dedicated space, sensory sensitivities are understood and respected, providing individuals with a safe and calming retreat where they can find solace and engage with their senses on their terms. The sensory room is a testament to the power of design to enhance the wellbeing of neurodiverse individuals by creating a sensory-friendly oasis and the opportunity to thrive in an environment tailored to their unique sensory experiences.

Minimalistic Design: A more minimalistic approach with minimised clutter can improve concentration and reduce sensory overload, especially for individuals with ADHD or autism. Desks or working spaces should be positioned away from windows, high-traffic areas, or busy artwork to minimise distractions.

Spatial Planning: Group related activities together to create functional and spatially organised areas. For example, you can design a reading nook with comfortable seating, suitable lighting, and book storage to support reading activities. Organised rooms that facilitate daily routines can provide reassurance for many individuals with neurodiverse conditions, especially those with ASD or dyslexia. If this area is within the living room, then use open bookcases to create a division without cluttering the space.

Optimising Layout and Organisation: Dyslexic individuals often benefit from clear and intuitive organisation. Designing spaces with straightforward layouts, well-defined zones, and logical flow can help reduce cognitive load. Furniture placement and spatial arrangement should promote effortless navigation within the home.

Noise and smell reduction: Use carpets, rugs, curtains, and wall-hanging accessories or art to minimise noise, benefiting individuals with sensory sensitivities to sounds. An open-plan kitchen and living area can be challenging for someone sensitive to smells or noise. In such cases, consider a separate kitchen to minimise both odours and noise.

Visual Cues: Individuals with cognitive challenges but thrive on clear structure can benefit from visual cues that help them identify different areas and objects within the home. Having an area with specific calendars featuring visual cues and easily identifiable organisers can be highly beneficial for some individuals with autism.

It's crucial to understand that neurodiversity is complex, with a wide range of needs, sensory sensitivities, and preferences. Consulting directly with the individual and their family, along with professionals who understand their needs, can provide valuable insights and help create a home that is beautiful and tailored to their specific requirements. Additionally, consulting a specialist in lighting design can ensure that lighting is optimised to meet individual sensitivities and preferences, creating a soothing and comfortable atmosphere.

For individuals with sensory sensitivities, the choice of tiles in interior spaces can play a crucial role in creating a comfortable and accommodating environment. Busy tiles, characterised by intricate patterns, bold colours, and contrasting textures, may pose challenges for those with sensory sensitivities. The visual complexity of busy tiles can be overwhelming and even distressing for some individuals, contributing to sensory overload and discomfort. In contrast, simpler and more neutral tiles, with their clean lines and muted colours, are often preferred by individuals with sensory sensitivities as they create a calmer and less stimulating environment. The choice of tiles can thus be a thoughtful consideration when designing spaces to be inclusive and accommodating for those with sensory sensitivities.

CHAPTER 14

Mental Health and Interior Design

Neurodiverse individuals commonly struggle with fitting into the social norms within their workplace or socially which can lead to prolonged stress, exhaustion, and in many cases mental health difficulties. The relationship between interior design and mental health is a topic of increasing importance and relevance, as people become more aware of how their living spaces can profoundly impact their psychological wellbeing. Thoughtfully designed interiors can contribute to mental health by promoting resilience and helping individuals cope with mental health challenges.

A design approach that can positively impact mental health is biophilic design. Biophilia, derived from the Greek words for "life" (bio) and "affinity" (philia), recognises the inherent human connection to nature. This design philosophy incorporates elements of nature into interior spaces, such as indoor plants, natural wood furnishings, and decor inspired by the natural world. By bringing the outdoors inside, biophilic design can reduce stress, enhance mood, and improve concentration. Alternatively, having greenery outside that is visible from the window can also create a soothing atmosphere.

Colour choices in interior design also play a significant role in affecting emotional responses. Colours can dictate the mood of a space and influence our feelings. For example, calming colours like blues and natural tones can reduce anxiety, while bright colours like red and yellows in small quantities and greens can promote happiness and energy. Selecting the right hues is crucial to creating a desired atmosphere.

Another aspect of interior design that can impact mental health is clutter. Cluttered spaces can increase stress, overwhelm, and anxiety. Embracing minimalist design

A window that seamlessly blends the outdoor greenery with the indoor space can evoke feelings of joy, serenity, and liberation.

principles can help reduce clutter, create a sense of order, and contribute to a more serene environment.

Personalisation is essential in interior design. Allowing individuals to incorporate cherished items, photographs, and beloved artwork into their living spaces can foster a sense of belonging and comfort. Personal touches can transform a house into a true home.

Open spaces in residential properties, like open-plan kitchens and living areas, can promote togetherness and communication. For families with members who have communication difficulties, creating well-defined spaces within these open areas can provide moments of retreat and solitude.

Acoustic considerations are vital in interior design. Poor acoustic design can lead to noise pollution, which can elevate stress levels, increase anxiety, disrupt sleep, and negatively impact overall wellbeing. Soft materials, soundproofing techniques, and strategic furniture placement can effectively manage and reduce noise levels, contributing to improved mental health.

Designing spaces for specific activities, such as reading nooks, relaxation corners, meditation areas, and hobby spaces, can enhance wellbeing and support various interests and needs.

In summary, the intersection of interior design and mental health underscores the significance of creating spaces that not only fulfil functional requirements but also nurture wellbeing and mental wellness. As awareness grows, more design professionals are integrating principles that cater to mental health into their projects, ultimately contributing to healthier and happier living environments for all.

CHAPTER 15

Fostering Inclusive Environments – Real-Life Illustrations

Inclusive design is crucial when considering the diverse needs and sensitivities of individuals within the neurodiverse community. Here are two case studies that highlight the importance of considering neurodiversity in design:

Sebastian's New Home

You met Sebastian who has significant sensory sensitivities. Sebastian had recently purchased a larger two-bedroom flat in a community complex, hoping to find a more spacious and communal living environment. However, he quickly became stressed due to the echoing noise in his new home, particularly the sounds from the flat below. Despite his initial excitement, Sebastian contemplated selling the property soon after he bought it, feeling overwhelmed.

Upon visiting Sebastian's new flat, it became clear that the issue was related to the design elements and furniture choices. The large kitchen, dining, and living area featured hardwood flooring, metal and glass furniture, leather seating, and glossy kitchen surfaces—all hard materials that contributed to sound reflection and amplification.

To address this, Sebastian was advised to invest in a larger carpet that covered most of the living area's flooring. This would help reduce noise by providing softness and padding. Although initially hesitant due to his preference for a clean and minimalistic look, Sebastian agreed.

Additionally, soft furnishings like cushions and a throw were added to his leather sofa, instantly transforming it into a cosy and inviting seating area. A squashy soft bean bag was placed in one of the corners of his living room for further relaxation.

Thick carpeting, blinds, and curtains can effectively minimise external noise.

To address the echoing issue, sheer curtains were installed, which not only reduced noise but also added a sense of warmth and comfort to the space without obstructing Sebastian's view of the surrounding gardens. Sebastian's love for hardwood flooring was accommodated by keeping the carpet limited to the living area.

By carefully selecting furnishings and materials to mitigate noise and create a comfortable environment, Sebastian's home was transformed into a serene and welcoming space that met his sensory needs and preferences.

Jane's studio

Jane, whom you met in the beginning of my book, lives in a studio in Central London and as I mention before she regularly works two days from home. Jane is very busy and she does not have much time to tidy her space, she needs clever storage to keep her studio tidy.

I created a small area which I separated from the rest of her studio with an open bookcase which has cupboards at the bottom half but not at the top half. Like this, I divided the area for her office space without making the space look smaller. I added a platform with storage under the bed and created a different level which worked well as it gives the illusion that the studio is larger. All curtains, bed cover and cushions were replaced with soft materials in light blue and light green. It is worth mentioning that the furniture is in off-white colour to make the studio lighter. Jane's studio now has three different areas which are well defined: a small dining / living area, an office area and a sleeping area. Jane is finally able to sleep well, she feels refreshed in the morning, and she loves working from home as she now has her dedicated office space. She also looks forward to going back home after a busy day at the company's office.

The key lies in creativity and resourcefulness, ensuring that small spaces not only meet but exceed their functionality expectations, proving that size is no limitation when it comes to effective design.

Each case study highlights the importance of taking a holistic approach to design, considering the unique needs, sensitivities, and preferences of individuals within the neurodiverse community. By integrating various design elements and flexible solutions, inclusive spaces can be created, promoting wellbeing and comfort for all residents, regardless of their cognitive, sensory, or physical characteristics.

PART III

PRACTICAL EXERCISES

CHAPTER 16

Understanding and Applying Neurodiverse-Friendly Design Principles

In this chapter, we will explore practical exercises that allow you to delve deeper into the world of neurodiverse-friendly interior design. As we have journeyed through the various aspects of neurodiverse-friendly interior design, we have gained valuable insights into the unique sensitivities, preferences, and needs of individuals within the neurodiverse community. Now, it's time to put this knowledge into practice through a series of engaging exercises. These exercises will not only enhance your understanding of the challenges faced by neurodiverse individuals but also equip you with the tools to design spaces that truly cater to their wellbeing.

The exercises in this chapter are designed to provide you with hands-on experience in comprehending the complex relationship between colour, sound, and lighting and their profound impact on the neurodiverse community. By actively participating in these exercises, you will gain a deeper appreciation of how design choices can affect emotions, behaviours, and sensory experiences.

We encourage you to approach these exercises with an open mind and a willingness to learn. Remember that neurodiversity is not a one-size-fits-all concept; each individual is unique. These exercises will help you develop the flexibility and adaptability needed to create spaces that cater to the specific needs and sensitivities of neurodiverse individuals.

So, let's dive into these practical exercises, exploring colour schemes, sound, and lighting, and discover how they can be harnessed to design more inclusive and supportive environments. By the end of this chapter, you'll be well-prepared to apply what you've learned in your own design projects, making a meaningful impact on the lives of neurodiverse individuals and their families.

Exercise 1: Reflection on Personal Experience

Explore your emotional reactions to different colours and reflect on how personal experiences and cultural influences may shape your perception.

In this exercise, we will look at the intricate relationship between colour, personal experiences, and cultural influences. By exploring your emotional reactions to various colours, you'll gain insight into how colour impacts your thoughts and feelings and develop a deeper understanding of neurodiverse perspectives.

Step 1: Colour Exploration

Begin by selecting a range of colours. You can do this by collecting colour swatches, using paint samples, or simply finding images of different colours online.

Take your time to study each colour individually. Observe how each one makes you feel emotionally and mentally. Do certain colours evoke strong emotions or memories? Note down your initial reactions.

Step 2: Personal Experiences

Now, consider your personal experiences related to each colour. Reflect on instances where you've encountered these colours in your life. Have you associated specific colours with positive or negative experiences? Perhaps a particular colour reminds you of a childhood bedroom, a favourite outfit, or a significant life event.

Step 3: Cultural Influences

Next, think about the cultural influences that may have shaped your perception of colour. Different cultures attach unique meanings and symbolism to colours. How have these cultural associations influenced your feelings towards certain colours? Are there cultural norms or traditions that have influenced your colour preferences?

Incorporating soothing blue colour tones into your surroundings can have a profound impact on the overall ambiance. This serene colour choice not only adds a sense of tranquillity but also promotes a feeling of relaxation and peace. Whether applied to interior walls, furniture, or decor accents, the use of calming blue hues creates an inviting and harmonious atmosphere that is conducive to wellbeing and comfort.

Step 4: Embracing Neurodiverse Perspectives

Now that you've explored your own reactions to colours, take a moment to consider how neurodiverse individuals might experience colours differently. Think about sensory sensitivities, such as heightened sensitivity to bright colours or aversion to certain colour combinations.

Imagine how personal experiences and cultural influences may affect neurodiverse individuals' perceptions of colour. This exercise encourages empathy and a broader understanding of diverse perspectives.

Step 5: Journal Your Insights

To conclude this exercise, journal your insights and reflections. Take note of any surprises or new realisations you've had about your own relationship with colour and how this exercise has deepened your understanding of neurodiversity.

This exercise is a valuable starting point for anyone interested in creating inclusive and sensory-friendly spaces for neurodiverse individuals. It fosters empathy and helps you recognise the importance of considering diverse perspectives in interior design.

Exercise 2: Exploring Neurodiverse Experiences

Engage in conversations with neurodiverse individuals about their colour preferences and other sensitivities. Get as much information as you can and find out why they feel the way they feel about the different colours. How do they feel about different noises and why. What about different smells and textures?

Step 1: Connect with Neurodiverse Individuals

Begin by identifying and connecting with neurodiverse individuals who are willing to share their experiences with you. These individuals may include those on the autism spectrum, individuals with sensory processing differences, or people with other neurodiverse needs.

Approach them respectfully and express your genuine interest in understanding their sensory experiences.

Step 2: Colour Preferences

Start by discussing colour preferences. Ask them about their favourite colours and why they are drawn to them. Inquire about colours they may find soothing or stimulating and the reasons behind those preferences.

Encourage them to share any specific memories or emotional connections they have with certain colours.

Step 3: Noise Sensitivities

Explore their sensitivities to noises. Inquire about sounds or noises that may trigger discomfort or anxiety and those that bring comfort or calmness.

Understand the reasons behind their reactions to different noises. For example, some neurodiverse individuals may be hypersensitive to loud sounds due to sensory processing differences.

Step 4: Smell Preferences

Discuss their reactions to different smells. Ask about scents they find pleasant, calming, or distressing.

Explore the potential associations between smells and past experiences that may influence their sensory responses.

Step 5: Texture Perceptions

Lastly, try to understand their perceptions of textures. Inquire about textures they find comforting, uncomfortable, or even painful.

Understand how their tactile sensitivities may impact their choices in clothing, furniture, and interior design.

Step 6: Active Listening

Throughout these conversations, practice active listening. Pay close attention to their words, feelings, and experiences validating their feelings and experiences, even if they differ from your own.

Step 7: Reflect and Learn

After engaging in these discussions, take time to reflect on what you've learned. Consider how the insights gained from neurodiverse individuals can inform your approach to inclusive interior design.

Recognise the importance of accommodating diverse sensory experiences in your design choices.

This exercise promotes a deeper understanding of neurodiverse perspectives and helping you create more inclusive and sensory-friendly interior designs that cater to a wider range of individuals' needs and preferences.

Exercise 3: Exploring the Impact of Colour in a Room

This exercise invites you to experiment with various colour schemes within a room in your home and observe how these choices can influence your mood and emotions. By actively participating in this hands-on exercise, you'll gain valuable insights into the powerful role that colour plays in shaping our interior environments.

Step 1: Select a Room

Choose a room in your home that you'd like to transform. It could be your living room, bedroom, or any space where you spend a significant amount of time.

Step 2: Explore Different Colour Schemes

Begin by selecting different colour schemes for the room. You can choose from monochromatic, complementary or analogous colour schemes, among others. Research the psychological effects of these colour combinations to guide your choices.

Step 3: Make the Changes

Introduce colour through furnishings, decor, and textiles based on the colour scheme you've selected. Ensure that each colour scheme is distinct and noticeable.

Step 4: Observe and Reflect

Spend time in the room under each different colour scheme. Pay close attention to how the colours make you feel emotionally and mentally. Are there specific emotions or moods that each colour scheme evokes?

Reflect on how the room's atmosphere changes with each colour scheme. Note any differences in your energy levels, relaxation, or overall wellbeing.

Step 5: Document Your Observations

Keep a journal or make notes of your observations and emotions associated with each colour scheme. Be specific in describing your experiences.

Step 6: Consider Practical Implications

Think about the practicality of each colour scheme. Did you find certain colour combinations more conducive to activities like work, relaxation, or socialising? Take note of any functional considerations.

Step 7: Share Your Findings

If possible, share your experiment with friends or family members and get their feedback on how the room's colours made them feel. Discuss any similarities or differences in your experiences.

Step 8: Reflect on Your Insights

After experimenting with various colour schemes, reflect on what you've learned about the profound impact of colour on our emotions and mood.

Consider how you can apply these insights to your interior design projects, especially when creating spaces that accommodate neurodiverse individuals' unique sensory needs and preferences.

This exercise provides a first-hand experience of the emotional and psychological effects of colour in interior design, offering valuable lessons for creating sensory-friendly and emotionally supportive environments for neurodiverse individuals.

Exercise 4: The Importance of Lighting

Experiment with various types of lighting in a space and observe how it influences the perception of colours.

This exercise encourages you to experiment with different types of lighting within a space and observe how it impacts the way colours are perceived. Lighting is a crucial element in interior design, and its effects on colour can be quite profound. By conducting this hands-on experiment, you'll gain insights into how lighting can shape the way we experience colour in our environments.

Step 1: Choose a Space

Select a room or area in your home where you can easily manipulate lighting conditions. It could be a living room, bedroom, or any space with a variety of light sources.

Step 2: Experiment with Lighting

Begin by varying the lighting in the chosen space. You can use natural light, overhead lighting, lamps, and different types of bulbs, such as warm and cool-toned LED lights.

Change the intensity and direction of the lighting to see how it affects the colours in the room.

Take note of how light enters the living room; in some situations, excessive light can be a disruptive element. Installing curtains or blinds that can be easily adjusted as needed is a very sensible choice.

Step 3: Observe Colour Perception

Spend time in the space under different lighting conditions. Take note of how the colours on walls, furniture, and decor items appear to change.

Pay attention to whether certain lighting conditions make colours appear more vibrant, subdued, warmer, or cooler.

Step 4: Document Your Observations

Keep a journal or make notes of your observations regarding how lighting influences colour perception. Describe any notable differences in how you perceive colours under various lighting scenarios.

Step 5: Consider Practical Implications

Think about the practical implications of your findings. For instance, how might different lighting choices affect the mood and functionality of a room?

Consider how you can use lighting strategically in interior design to enhance or modify the perception of colours to create specific atmospheres.

Step 6: Share Your Experiment

If possible, share your experiment and findings with others, such as family members or friends, and gather their perspectives on how lighting influenced their perception of colours.

Step 7: Reflect on Your Insights

Reflect on what you've learned about the significant role of lighting in shaping our perception of colour in interior spaces.

Consider how this knowledge can inform your approach to designing sensory-friendly environments for neurodiverse individuals, where lighting choices play a crucial role in creating comfortable and visually appealing settings.

This exercise provides valuable first-hand experience in understanding how lighting can transform our perception of colours within interior spaces. It highlights the importance of thoughtful lighting design in creating sensory-friendly and emotionally supportive environments for neurodiverse individuals.

Exercise 5: Sensory Sensitivities

Explore how sound impacts your senses by listening to soft and loud music and engaging in activities that create noise.

This exercise invites you to explore how sound influences your sensory experiences by experimenting with different auditory stimuli, including soft and loud music, as well as activities that create varying levels of noise. By actively engaging in this sensory experiment, you'll gain a deeper understanding of how sound can affect individuals with sensory sensitivities, including those who are neurodiverse.

Step 1: Create a Quiet Environment

Begin by setting up a quiet and comfortable space where you can focus on auditory experiences without distractions.

Step 2: Soft Music Experiment

Start with soft, calming music. Play it at a low volume and listen attentively. Observe how this gentle music affects your mood, relaxation, and overall sense of comfort. Note any physical or emotional responses you experience while listening.

Step 3: Loud Music Experiment

Transition to louder, more energetic music. Increase the volume and engage with this music for a period of time. Take note of how it impacts your emotions, energy levels, and overall sensory experiences.

Reflect on any differences you notice between the soft and loud music experiments.

Step 4: Engage in Noisy Activities

To further explore sound's impact, engage in activities that create varying levels of noise. This could include activities like cooking with sizzling pans, vacuuming, opening and closing cupboards or even tapping on a keyboard.

Pay attention to how these noisy activities affect your sensory sensitivities and overall comfort.

Step 5: Reflect and Document

Keep a journal or make notes of your observations throughout the experiments. Describe how the different auditory experiences made you feel and any physical or emotional sensations you encountered.

Reflect on the potential implications of these experiences for individuals with sensory sensitivities, especially those who are neurodiverse.

Step 6: Share Your Insights

If appropriate, discuss your experiments with friends or family members and gather their perspectives on how sound influences their sensory experiences.

Step 7: Apply Your Knowledge

Consider how the insights gained from this exercise can inform your approach to designing interior spaces that accommodate individuals with sensory sensitivities. Think about how you can create quieter and more sensory-friendly environments.

This exercise provides a first hand understanding of how sound can impact sensory sensitivities and offers valuable insights into the experiences of neurodiverse individuals who may have heightened sensitivity to noise. It underscores the importance of designing spaces that consider these sensory factors to promote comfort and wellbeing.

Exercise 6: Apply What You Learned in Practice

Design a room in your home with the sensitivities and needs of a neurodiverse individual in mind, considering their preferences and sensory sensitivities.

In this exercise, you'll put your knowledge to practical use by designing a room in your home with the specific sensitivities and needs of a neurodiverse individual in mind. By considering their preferences and sensory sensitivities, you'll gain hands-on experience in creating an inclusive and accommodating interior space.

Step 1: Choose a Room

Select a room in your home where you'd like to implement sensory-friendly design. It could be a bedroom, a quiet study area, or any space where an individual may need a sensory-friendly environment.

Step 2: Research and Planning

Begin by researching the specific sensory needs and sensitivities of neurodiverse individuals who may use the space. This may involve considering factors such as colour preferences, lighting preferences, noise reduction, and tactile comfort.

Plan your design based on the gathered information and insights.

Step 3: Colour and Lighting

Choose a colour scheme that aligns with the preferences of the neurodiverse individual. Consider calming and soothing colours, taking into account any aversions they may have.

Implement appropriate lighting, incorporating natural light when possible and selecting lighting fixtures that can be adjusted for brightness and warmth.

Step 4: Furniture and Layout

Select furniture that prioritises comfort and functionality. Avoid sharp edges or overly complex designs.

Plan the room layout to create clear and uncluttered pathways, making it easier to navigate for individuals with sensory sensitivities.

Step 5: Sensory Elements

Introduce sensory elements that cater to the individual's needs. This could include soft textiles, tactile surfaces, and cosy seating options.

Incorporate sensory tools or devices that may benefit them, such as weighted blankets or fidget toys.

Step 6: Noise Reduction

Implement strategies for noise reduction in the room. This might involve using sound-absorbing materials, adding curtains or blinds to dampen outside noise, or creating a quiet corner for relaxation.

Step 7: Personalisation

Allow for personalisation of the space. Consider incorporating elements that reflect the individual's interests and preferences, such as artwork, decor, or hobbies.

Step 8: Test and Adjust

Once the room is set up, spend time in it to test its functionality and comfort. Pay attention to how well it meets the sensory needs and preferences you identified earlier.

Be prepared to make adjustments as needed based on your observations.

Step 9: Reflect and Learn

Reflect on your experience designing a sensory-friendly room and consider how this exercise has deepened your understanding of creating inclusive environments.

Recognise the importance of thoughtful and empathetic design in accommodating the needs of neurodiverse individuals.

By completing these exercises, you'll gain valuable insights into the world of neurodiverse-friendly interior design and be better equipped to create inclusive and supportive spaces. We now understand better the value of inclusivity and tailored design and the importance of continued research, collaboration and professional training to further advance this field.

Let's apply what we've learned to make a positive impact on the lives of neurodiverse individuals and their families.

PART IV

CULTIVATING NEURODIVERSE-INCLUSIVE DESIGN: RESEARCH, LITERATURE REVIEW, AND INSPIRATIONAL CASE STUDIES

CHAPTER 17

Research and Literature Review

The field of interior design has evolved significantly over the years, expanding its focus from aesthetics and practicality to embrace inclusivity, with particular attention to neurodiversity. This chapter highlights some information available from existing research, examining the crucial role of interior design in enhancing the lives of the neurodiverse community.

"A Case Study on the Effect of Light and Colours in the Built Environment on Autistic Children's Behaviour" 2022.

This comprehensive case study, conducted by a collaborative team of researchers led by Ashwini Sunil Nair and her colleagues from the School of Architecture and Interior Design at SRM Institute of Science and Technology in Chennai, India, in collaboration with experts from Xuzhou Medical University in China and University Malaya in Kuala Lumpur, Malaysia, studies the dynamics of how colour, light, sound, and space significantly influence the behaviour and experiences of autistic children within built environments. Notably, the study adopts an in depth approach using real life examples to demonstrate that for autistic children who perceive colours with heightened intensity, making colour choices within interior spaces is pivotal to their wellbeing. The study emphasises the judicious selection of colours, favouring autism-friendly palettes such as pastel shades, neutral tones, and muted hues. It underscores the potential of these colours to create a calming and sensory-friendly atmosphere. Conversely, bold and vibrant colours are cautioned against, as they can lead to overstimulation and heightened agitation among autistic children, who may already grapple with self-confidence issues and adaptability challenges.

The study's exploration of lighting illustrates the interplay between light and colour and their profound physiological effects on autistic children. It endorses overhead lighting as the preferred option, primarily due to its minimal direct eye-level visibility. Whenever possible, prioritise direct lighting and natural daylighting over intense light or glare in various settings. The research emphasises that lighting considerations extend beyond the selection of light sources, extending to the regulation of light levels through dimmer switches. This approach allows for personalised adjustments, catering to the unique sensory sensitivities of individual autistic children.

In terms of spatial organisation, the study highlights the significance of creating well-defined and orderly spaces tailored to the routines and predictability that autistic children often crave. It advocates for clear, accessible, and inclusive environments, acknowledging that spatial layouts directly impact how autistic children navigate and interact within these spaces.

Furthermore, the study underscores the pivotal role of sound in the sensory experience of autistic individuals. It asserts that lower sound levels, below 50 dB, are conducive to an autism-friendly environment, whereas sound levels exceeding 60 dB can lead to the manifestation of inappropriate behaviours. This finding emphasises the importance of considering auditory stimuli when designing spaces for autistic children.

In conclusion, this research concludes the holistic significance of light, colour, sound, and space in creating environments that cater to the unique sensory needs of autistic children. It calls for a sensory-sensitive approach to design, aiming to provide positive sensory experiences and enhance the overall wellbeing of autistic individuals. By recognising and implementing these critical variables effectively, designers can contribute to the development of inclusive and supportive environments that empower and nurture autistic children.

Built Environment Design and People with Autism Spectrum Disorder (ASD): A Scoping Review, 2021

The research conducted by Giulia Tola, Valentina Talu, Tanja Congiu, Paul Bain, and Jutta Lindert from the Department of Architecture, Design, and Planning at the University of Sassari in Italy delves into the pivotal role of built environment design in improving the quality of life for individuals with Autism Spectrum Disorder (ASD). This scoping review undertakes an exhaustive examination of the existing body of literature pertaining to the intricate relationship between individuals with

ASD and the built environment, particularly within the context of creating spaces that are conducive to the wellbeing of individuals with autism.

The review discerns and underscores three core factors that are imperative when considering the architectural design of spaces accommodating individuals with ASD: sensory quality, intelligibility, and predictability of the built environment. For each of these factors, the authors offer comprehensive insights into spatial prerequisites that are essential in addressing the unique requirements of individuals with ASD. While much of the research in this field has concentrated on designing autism-friendly educational spaces, particularly tailored to schoolchildren with ASD, this study brings to light the relatively limited attention devoted to examining the interface between the built environment and adults with ASD, with a notable emphasis on residential settings.

By scrutinising and synthesising existing knowledge, this research contributes to a deeper understanding of how architectural design can be harnessed to foster a more inclusive and supportive environment for individuals with ASD across various life stages. The insights derived from this scoping review hold the potential to inform future design practices, offering architects, planners, and policy makers valuable guidelines to create environments that promote the wellbeing and integration of individuals with ASD into society.

"The Effect of the Home Environment on Children with Autism Spectrum Disorder", 2023

The research was conducted by a collaborative team from Cyprus. This study aimed to investigate how the home environment influences the behaviour of children with ASD, as perceived by their mothers.

The research findings revealed that mothers identified factors such as reducing clutter, ensuring the presence of safe and durable materials in the home, and utilising sensory rooms as having a positive influence on their autistic children's behaviour.

Additionally, mothers put forth a range of suggestions for an ideal home environment, including the creation of relaxation corners, the provision of dedicated spaces for visual schedules, ensuring ample storage areas to prevent clutter, and offering safe indoor and outdoor play environments. They also emphasised the significance of personal space, the need for a "quiet room" for calming down, and the use of durable household materials.

The study underscored the critical importance of establishing a safe and secure home environment for autistic children. This included simple changes like providing quiet spaces and spacious living areas while minimising safety hazards.

In terms of recommendations, the study suggests that parents should actively seek help and support when their child receives a diagnosis of ASD to access available treatments and services. It is crucial for parents to understand and address triggers for challenging behaviours in their autistic children, which involves adapting the environment to reduce stressors.

Furthermore, the study highlights the significance of acceptance and unconditional love in ensuring the wellbeing of children with autism. It encourages parents to embrace their child's uniqueness and persistently support their growth and development throughout their life journey.

In summary, this research sheds light on the pivotal role played by the home environment in shaping the behaviour and well-being of autistic children. The findings provide valuable insights into specific adaptations that can enhance the quality of life for these children, with the aim of guiding professionals and parents in providing effective support and care.

CHAPTER 18

Existing Designs that Showcase the Importance of Neurodiverse-Inclusive Design Principles

Maggie's Centres across the UK: These centres provide a calming environment that integrates biophilic design principles, striking a balance between nature and architectural design, which is particularly beneficial for neurodiverse individuals.

Sydney Neurology Clinic: This medical facility offers a calming, inviting, and warm environment that departs from the traditional clinical setting. It showcases thoughtful design aimed at providing a positive experience for patients.

The Sheffield Autism Research Laboratory at the University of Sheffield: This laboratory is clearly designed to meet the needs of the neurodiverse population, featuring adaptable spaces and predictable layouts.

While exemplary designs exist which demonstrate the advantages of inclusive environments, various challenges persist. These include a lack of awareness, resistance to change, and cost considerations, which often favour the status quo in design practices that cater to the majority rather than the neurodiverse community.

The emergence of the COVID-19 pandemic introduced unforeseen challenges, necessitating creative solutions and innovative responses in the field of interior design.

Notably, there is very little research related to residential homes for the neurodiverse community, highlighting the need for further exploration in this area.

In conclusion, interior design has a pivotal role to play in creating inclusive spaces that benefit individuals with neurodiverse conditions. Despite challenges, increased awareness and continued research can lead to a more inclusive and accommodating design landscape that prioritises the wellbeing and needs of all individuals.

Mood boards, a fundamental tool in the realm of design, are instrumental in articulating and visualizing creative visions.

CONCLUSION

In the journey to create inclusive and accommodating spaces for the neurodiverse population, it is imperative to recognise that each individual is unique, with their own set of needs, sensitivities, and preferences. Flexibility and adaptability in design are key to crafting environments that truly support neurodiversity.

It's crucial to understand that neurodiverse conditions are not disorders to be fixed or cured. Rather, they represent natural variations in the human experience, and individuals with these conditions possess unique abilities and strengths that can contribute significantly to society.

Moving forward, there are several important steps to take:

Raising Awareness: It is essential for the broader community, including designers and architects, to understand the importance of tailored and inclusive design for the neurodiverse population, not only in residential settings but also in workplaces and public areas.

Research: While there has been some research in this field, more comprehensive studies are needed to gain a deeper understanding of the specific needs and preferences of the neurodiverse community and how these impact daily life. This research should inform the development of new design styles that support neurodiversity while benefiting everyone.

Adaptability and Customisation: Design should avoid a one-size-fits-all approach. Spaces should be adaptable to allow individuals to make adjustments based on their comfort levels and sensory sensitivities. Inclusive design should aim to be comfortable and accommodating for all in the household or school and work environment.

Ongoing Review: Regularly assess and monitor the effectiveness of existing and new designs. Make necessary adjustments based on feedback from individuals and emerging research.

Technology Integration: Leverage technology to create customisable and adaptable environments that can meet a variety of needs and preferences. Incorporate global design trends, technology advancements, and social awareness into the design process.

Involvement of the Neurodiverse Individual: The active participation of neurodiverse individuals in the design process is paramount. Their insights and feedback ensure that sensitivities, needs, and preferences are effectively addressed.

Professional Training: Training for interior designers and other professionals involved in the design process to equip them with the knowledge and skills needed to create neurodiverse-friendly environments efficiently and effectively.

Collaboration: Collaborate with specialists, including healthcare professionals, occupational therapists, psychologists, and educational institutions, to integrate effective design elements into living spaces. These partnerships can lead to practical, calming, and healing interiors that truly feel like home for the neurodiverse community.

By working together, sharing knowledge, and embracing collaboration, we can create a future where inclusive design becomes the norm, empowering individuals with neurodiverse conditions to thrive in spaces that support their unique needs and promote their wellbeing.

APPENDICES

Glossary related to neurodiversity and interior design

Achromatic Colour: Colours that lack hue, such as black, white, and shades of grey. These colours are often used in interior design for their neutral and calming qualities.

Acoustic Design: The planning and implementation of sound-related elements in interior spaces to optimise acoustics, including reducing noise, enhancing sound quality, and minimising sound distractions.

Biophilic Design: An approach to interior design that incorporates elements of nature, such as plants, natural light, and materials, to improve wellbeing and connection to the environment.

Chroma: The purity or intensity of a colour, often referred to as its saturation or vividness. Colours with high chroma are more vibrant, while those with low chroma are subdued.

Circadian Rhythm: The body's natural internal clock that regulates sleep-wake cycles and other physiological processes over a 24-hour period. Proper lighting design can support a healthy circadian rhythm.

Colour Temperature: A measure of the warmth or coolness of light, typically measured in Kelvin (K). Warmer light has lower colour temperatures, while cooler light has higher colour temperatures.

Colour Theory: Colour theory is the study of how colours work together. It involves concepts like the colour wheel, primary, secondary, and tertiary colours, complementary and analogous colour pairs, warm and cool colours, and colour harmony.

Understanding these principles helps artists and designers create visually pleasing combinations and convey emotions through colour choices. Colour theory is a fundamental tool in various creative fields, guiding decisions on colour selection and composition for effective visual.

Decoupling: A method in soundproofing design that involves separating building materials to prevent sound transmission, reducing noise between spaces.

Diffuser: An acoustic element or device used to scatter sound waves in different directions, reducing echoes and creating a more even sound distribution in a room.

Dystonia: Dystonia is a neurological disorder characterized by involuntary muscle contractions that lead to abnormal movements or postures.

Ergonomics: The study of designing spaces and products to optimize human comfort, safety, and efficiency. In interior design, ergonomic principles are applied to create user-friendly and accessible spaces.

LED: An LED, or Light Emitting Diode, is like a tiny electronic gadget that can make light when electricity flows through it. Think of it as a little light bulb, but much smaller and more efficient. LEDs are used in lots of things, like the little lights on your phone or computer, traffic signals, and even in regular light bulbs at home.

Neurodiversity: The concept that neurological differences, such as autism, ADHD, and sensory processing disorders, are natural variations of the human brain and should be recognized and respected.

Resilient Channels: Metal or flexible channels used in soundproofing to isolate walls or ceilings, preventing sound transmission between spaces.

Sensory Processing Disorder (SPD): A condition where the brain has difficulty processing and responding to sensory information from the environment.

Soft Materials: Materials with sound-absorbing properties, often used in interior design to reduce noise levels and echoes, including carpets, drapes, and upholstered furniture.

Soundproofing: The process of reducing or eliminating sound transmission between spaces, making an interior environment quieter and more comfortable.

Visual Sensory Sensitivity: Heightened sensitivity to visual stimuli, such as bright lights, patterns, or colours, commonly experienced by neurodiverse individuals.

VOC: It stands for "Volatile Organic Compounds." VOCs are a group of chemical compounds that can easily evaporate into the air at room temperature. These compounds can be found in various products, including paints, solvents, cleaning agents, and some building materials. When VOCs evaporate into the air, they can contribute to air pollution and have the potential to harm human health and the environment. Common examples of VOCs include formaldehyde, benzene, and acetone. Efforts are made to limit VOC emissions in various industries to reduce their negative impact on air quality and health.

Resources and recommendations for professional assistance:

1. ADHD Foundation (adhdfoundation.org.uk)

   The ADHD Foundation Neurodiversity Charity is the largest provider of training in ADHD and neurodevelopmental conditions for professionals in the UK.

2. Sensory Trust (sensorytrust.org.uk)

   An organization focused on creating sensory-friendly environments, with resources and case studies.

3. Tourette's Action (tourettes-action.org.uk)

   This organisation is a support and research charity working to improve the lives of people living with Tourette Syndrome.

4. National Autistic Society (autism.org.uk)

   Leading Charity for autistic people and their families. It has been providing support, guidance and advice since 1962.

5. Autism Speaks (autismspeaks.org)

   An advocacy organization with information on sensory-friendly design and resources for families.

6. National Autism Association (nationalautismassociation.org)

   Offers resources and information on creating sensory-friendly spaces for individuals with autism.

7. British Sleep Society (sleepsociety.org.uk)

   The British Sleep Society (BSS) is a professional organisation for medical, scientific and healthcare workers dealing with sleeping disorders.

8. British Dyslexia Association (bdadyslexia.org.uk)

   The British Dyslexia Association (BDA) has been advocating for individuals with dyslexia since 1972 and striving to create a dyslexia-friendly society accessible to all.

9. Dyspraxia Foundation (dyspraxiafoundation.org.uk)

   The Foundation provides support to parents, individuals, and professionals who either live with dyspraxia or support those affected by it.

ACKNOWLEDGEMENTS

I am grateful to my mother for instilling her enthusiasm and her caring nature into me, and to my father for his teachings that emphasised good values and kindness, his guidance that taught me to be brave. Special thanks also go to my Godfather, who encouraged me to dream big and believe in myself. Thank you to my sister, who consistently motivates me to strive for self-improvement.

To all my beloved family and friends in Greece, I want to express my gratitude for their encouragement, support, and unconditional love. Their belief in me has been a driving force, pushing me to reach for my dreams and pursue my goals. The support they've shown me, both in good times and challenging moments means the world to me.

I am eternally grateful to my cherished friends Dr Mirna Jovicic and Igor Vasilev, for their encouragement and support. Their presence in my life has been a constant source of strength and guidance. Their friendship is a treasure that I hold dear.

I extend my gratitude to Dr Riyaad Sayed, a great friend whose consistent encouragement throughout the years of our friendship has been a constant source of inspiration and support.

Thank you to my esteemed colleagues at the Centre for Interventional Paediatric Psychopharmacology and Rare Diseases at Maudsley Hospital, led by Professor Paramala Santosh, to my dedicated co-workers at the Hillingdon Child Development Centre, to my invaluable colleagues at The Children's Trust in Tadworth and to my compassionate colleagues at the Cheyne Child Development Unit at Chelsea and Westminster Hospital. Each one of them has played an instrumental role in enriching my knowledge and professional growth, often in ways that may have gone unnoticed but have been truly invaluable.

Furthermore, I would like to express my appreciation to two of my dear friends, Dr Remus Florea and Tudor Cosop, for their insightful suggestions and support throughout this journey. Their willingness to contribute their wisdom has made this endeavour all the more special.

I want to express my gratitude to Dr John O'Connell, my mentor, whose role in my medical career cannot be overstated. Dr O'Connell's guidance has instilled in me a deep understanding of the vital importance of humility in our noble profession and his generosity in sharing his experience has been an invaluable resource throughout my journey.

I want to extend my profound gratitude to both Philipp Engelmann and Dr Pui Yin Kwan for their invaluable contributions and suggestions that have significantly enhanced the quality and impact of my book. I am truly thankful for their dedication and the positive influence they have had on this project.

I would like to express my heartfelt gratitude to Rebecca Weir for her profound and uplifting encouragement. Her kindness in extending her support and knowledge, even to a complete stranger like me at the time, has left an enduring impression that I cherish deeply.

I am also deeply thankful to Rebecca's team at Light IQ and Contractors Rigby and Rigby for generously providing the photos featured in Chapter 11 (pages 52 and 54). **Photo Credit- Contractors Rigby and Rigby- Design By Taylor Howes.**

I am indebted to Peggy McColl for her support and invaluable guidance that has been instrumental throughout my journey as an author. Her expertise, mentorship, and genuine commitment to my success have not only enriched my writing but also empowered me to reach new heights in the literary world. Peggy's guidance has been a beacon of inspiration, offering insights that have transformed my writing and approach to publishing. I am immensely grateful for her generous spirit.

I want to express my gratitude to Hasmark Publishing International for their outstanding dedication and expertise in bringing my book to life. Their exceptional work and support have played a great role in making my dream of publishing a reality. I am truly thankful for their contributions and the remarkable team they have.

Many thanks to my photographer, Anna Stathaki. All photos showcasing my designs have been captured through her lenses, with the exception of those on pages 52 and 54. Thank you to Boutique Stone for arranging and generously sponsoring the photo shoot of my design featured on page 38.

A special thank you to Dr Catlin Neill and Dr Sophie Grant for sharing their ideas with me. Thank you to my good friend Sapho Diamanti for her valuable suggestions.

And last but not least, a big thank you to Sharon Stammers and her team at Women in Lighting, for sharing their knowledge, which holds immense value to me. I am forever grateful for these acts of kindness.

Sales Page

Neurodiversity-Inclusive Interior Design Course: Empowering Diversity through Design

Experience the transformational power of specialised training for interior designers. This program empowers designers with the profound knowledge and practical skills needed to champion neurodiversity and implement inclusive design principles. Explore a world of design that goes beyond comfort to empower, ensuring spaces that not only support individual needs but also celebrate strengths. Unveil the strategies that will revolutionise your design approach, forging spaces that are not just accommodating but liberating for the neurodiverse community.

Other written books:

Charlie and Martha Monkeys, a Magical Medicine Journey

"Charlie and Martha Monkeys: A Magical Medicine Journey" is a heart-warming children's book crafted by the collaborative efforts of Dr Maria Xirou and Racheal Porteous, a dedicated Paediatric Nurse. With their extensive knowledge and years of experience, they have masterfully created a captivating tale that not only engages young readers but also serves as a valuable tool to assist children in taking their medicines. This enchanting storybook has garnered widespread acclaim, resonating with children from around the globe, and stands as a testament to Dr Maria Xirou and Rachael Porteous's commitment to the wellbeing and comfort of young patients everywhere.

Upcoming books:

Revive: Interior Design for Brain Injury Recovery

In the wake of a brain injury, the environment plays a crucial role in the recovery journey. 'Revive: Interior Design for Brain Injury Recovery' explores how thoughtful interior design can foster healing, comfort, and a renewed sense of wellbeing. Discover expert insights and practical solutions that transform living spaces into therapeutic havens, promoting not only physical recovery but also emotional and mental wellbeing. This book is your guide to creating environments that empower individuals on their path to recovery, offering hope and inspiration for a brighter future.

Useful Information

Website: http://xiroukatyalinteriors.com

Instagram: @xiroukatyal.interiors

LinkedIn: Maria Xirou

Email address: maria@xiroukatyalinteriors.com

www.ingramcontent.com/pod-product-compliance
Lightning Source LLC
Chambersburg PA
CBHW040714220426
43209CB00091B/1839